JUNK SALE

JUNK SALE

STORIES & ESSAYS

PATRICK LOMBARDI

New Jersey

Second Paperback Edition, August 2021

The *Stories* in this book are a work of fiction. Names, characters, places, and incidents are either the product of the author's imagination or, if real, used fictitiously.

The *Essays* in this book depict actual events. Names and characteristics may have been altered to protect the identity of the individuals.

patricklombardi.com

Cover designed by Hortasar Covers

ISBN-13: 978-1722633363
ISBN-10: 1722633360

Printed in the United States of America

CONTENTS

STORIES

ESSAYS

STORIES

The Catcher in the Park

"Do you wanna get married?" I ask her this as she sits down next to me. The bench is splintered and covered in yellow pollen, but she doesn't seem to mind.

"What?" She looks confused. Why do women always look confused when I ask them that?

"I asked if you wanna get married."

She doesn't answer right away. A breeze pushes her long, brown hair into her eyes as she stares at me, and she begins tying it into a bun.

"I don't even *know* you," she says after a few seconds. A bit of an attitude on this one. I like that.

"All the more reason," I say.

That's when she grabs her purse and jacket and hurries away, disgusted. Probably with me.

Central Park's enormous. So you figure if you plop yourself down on a park bench and ask random women to marry you enough times, one of them is bound to say yes.

Not for Holden Caulfield.

That's not really my name. But if I told you my actual name, would it really make a difference?

I can sense you're already getting fed up with me. That's, like, my sixth sense—I can sense when people are getting fed up with me. I sense that a lot.

I can especially sense it when I ask just another beautiful girl to marry me. You think they'd be flattered. But nope. Not with me. I'm just another Holden Caulfield.

See what I did there?

No, but seriously: The real reason I'm sitting out here by myself on this gorgeous sunny day is because I'm waiting for someone. Not just any-one—*the* one. She's beautiful, funny, smart, out-going, and doesn't get disgusted when I ask her to marry me. In fact, it's that very question that draws her to me. Maybe she's just desperate to get mar-ried—the monotony of her single life mixed with her incessantly increasing age is driving her nuts. Or maybe she just can't resist my devilishly hand-some looks and infinite supply of ripped jeans and faded band T-shirts. Whatever it is, I don't care, and I'd hate to offend her by asking.

So on this fantastic day, when the clouds are finally sharing the sky with the sun, I wait for her.

As I'm waiting and daydreaming, she sits down next to me, in the void the last one left. The day is warming up, and she removes her red zippered sweatshirt. I love that sweatshirt. Her long, dirty blonde hair gets tangled in the hood, but she untangles it with a gentle tug, like a pro. She places her sweatshirt in the space between us and finally makes eye contact with me.

So I ask, "Do you wanna get married?"

She scrunches her nose and squints her eyes, sizing me up. I can even make out a slight smirk. But once she realizes I'm not joking, her upper lip twitches and she grabs her sweatshirt and stomps away to another bench, far away from me.

Nope. Not her.

Prized Possessions

When I was a kid, my mother always used to tell me not to steal.

"If you steal something," she would say, "that thing will bring you bad luck."

I believed her, of course. Little kids don't mess with bad luck. But then when I was ten years old, I acquired a miniature Buzz Lightyear action figure from my friend's house. I had the same exact one, and I thought he had stolen it from me. He pleaded that he hadn't, but I knew it was mine. So I took it back.

I brought it up to my bedroom to put it back on the shelf with my other *Toy Story* figures, but there he was; Buzz Lightyear—*mine*—was on that shelf, right there between Woody and the Slinky dog. My friend's toy was still in my hand.

I wondered how many other ten-year-olds

were faced with this same dilemma. Do I go back and apologize? Or do I keep Buzz and pretend he was mine? I chose the latter. After all, a kid can never have too many *Toy Story* collectables.

If you're wondering whether or not I still have those two identical action figures nineteen years later, the answer is yes. I'd be a fool to throw them away, especially considering that day was a turning point in my life. I had found out that the things you take do not actually bring you bad luck, which is great, because I love to take things. But don't call me a kleptomaniac. I'm not insane. I'm not like one of those pyromaniacs who wants to start fires everywhere he goes—although I *have* been taking a lot of candles and long-reach matches and crap like that lately. Something about being so close to objects that can cause so much destruction just drives me wild. But that's not the point. I just enjoy the thrill of taking something that isn't mine. It's not just the thrill of *taking* something though—it's the way I feel *before* I do. That pounding in my chest, like a kick drum pedal beating against the inside of my chest plate, when I see a souvenir mug or dusty antique book. I don't know that I want it until I see it, and then I know right away. It's great when the items easily fit into your pockets, but it's even better when they don't. Then your heart beats faster as you try to conceal it under a skin-tight T-shirt or in the leg of a bulky pair of jeans. Each step brings you closer to getting caught, but when you finally make it to your room, alone and sweaty, you can breathe, and update your collection.

That's the sort of thrill I relish. I'm not a psychopath.

Lately, I've enjoyed sifting through people's homes when they're not around. It's like wandering through the aisles of a Burlington Coat Factory. I find it funny how many people leave their living room windows unlocked. That's where I try first, because that's usually the best way to get in. Maybe it's a warm night when you're sitting on your couch watching TV, so you open the window to let in a cool breeze. At night before you go to bed, or in the morning while you're rushing to work, you close the window, but you forget to lock it.

Thank you for that, I say.

I don't take much whenever I roam through someone's home. Like I said, I don't *need* to. I don't know where a person's most valuable possessions are kept; I can't tell you where families hide their safes; I'm not sure how to tell which electronics wrack up the most bucks. No, I go for the objects out in the open—picture frames, clocks, artwork—objects that sit idle for years, barely even looked at by their owners. I've built a collection of things I have no use for because these families have no use for them either. I look at myself as a "de-clutterer," not a thief.

The last home I visited had too little clutter, though, and that made the thrill so much more exhilarating.

I climbed in through a window in the back of a house with peach-colored siding all around the exterior. I fell into what I thought was a living room, but it couldn't have been—there was no TV. There wasn't a rug either, only wood floors, polished and looking brand new like an exhibit at a museum. The entire interior of the home had a slightly orange tint to it, like it was perpetually sunset in the middle of September. I felt warm, even though the air conditioner didn't stop running as long as I was there.

I don't have a method. I don't go to the bedroom first and work my way through the living spaces. Nothing like that. I let the homes guide *me*, and for some reason, this house guided me toward picture frames. There were photos all throughout the house—on the walls, on side tables, on the mantle above the fireplace—but none of them were of people. Each frame held the photo of some beautiful landscape. There were oceans, deserts, waterfalls, sunsets, farms, cities, and so many more places I wished to be. Each one was so stunning that I didn't know which one to take.

I walked up a solid wooden staircase with exactly eighteen steps, eleven of them creaking underneath my feet. The second floor split into two sections, and I turned right. There was a bedroom, the door ajar, at the end of the long hallway. The first thing I noticed about it when I stepped inside was the lack of furniture. The bed, which was next to the door, faced one dresser on the opposite wall, right next to the room's sole window. Besides that, there was no other furniture. No desk, no nightstand, no chairs. But there *were* shelves, exactly fourteen of them. They lined all four of the bedroom walls. Each one was cluttered with trophies and medals and ribbons, some for swimming, some for soccer, some for field hockey, and a number of other sports.

I walked up to one shelf, the one right above the dresser. It held six trophies, one blue ribbon, and a gold medal without the neck ribbon attached. The awards were in no particular order, as far as I could tell. They looked like they were organized by an old man with cataracts and Parkinson's. I slid the side of my index finger across the front edge of the shelf. Not a speck of dust, as if the shelf was wiped clean this morning.

The trophies were extravagant. Each one on this shelf was at least a foot tall, supported by a thick, square base. One of them, though—the second from the left—was for football. The helmeted figure on top was most certainly male. Every other trophy on this shelf, and seemingly all the shelves, displayed figures of females. I was sure this one was a mistake, or perhaps just the way things are. I imagined she was the only female on her high school football team, and they only made male figures for football trophies.

I thought about picking it up, taking it home, but I dropped my hand back down to my side. I looked down at the dresser in front of me. Just like the shelf, it too was spotless. The dresser itself, no more than four feet high and six feet wide, held only two items: a small, wooden jewelry box and a square picture frame. The frame was support for the photograph inside, as picture frames typically are, but the frame supported the photo in more ways than one.

The frame was painted so thick in white that it almost looked plastic. Red hearts sat in each corner. Inside the frame was a photograph of a man and a woman. The man had his arm around her waist. From memory, I couldn't tell you what the man looked like—I think he had short black hair—but the woman, her smile was radiant. Her long, frizzy blood red hair was draped over one shoulder. Strands seemed to be blowing in her freckled face. She had as many freckles as I did, and it made me smile. Her eyes looked blue, or they could have been a light green, but either way, they were staring right at me.

As I was gawking at her photo, I heard a bit of commotion coming from downstairs, and I froze in place, holding my breath and squeezing my eyes shut. The front door slammed, and footsteps stomped along the linoleum.

"I thought I closed this dang window," I heard a man's voice say.

I turned back to the photo, grabbed it, and tried to fit it into my side pocket. It was too large, so I lifted my shirt and slid it between my back and the waistband of my jeans. I creeped out of the bedroom and felt the frame jab my lower back with every step.

Here it was. The thrill. The increased heart rate. The beads of sweat forming at the peak of my forehead and under my arms. I had to find a way out without getting caught. I told myself that several times.

I stood at the top of the staircase and held my breath and listened again. No sounds. At the bottom of the staircase was the front door, a set of keys still in the deadbolt. Once I had an idea of where that man was, I could make my way down the steps and flee through the front door. I assumed it didn't matter whether I ran or stepped lightly, because nearly a dozen steps would have squealed like pigs even at my stealthiest.

I heard a shuffle come from below. A plate dropped. Then running water. He must have been in the kitchen. I had no idea where the kitchen was, but this was the opportunity I had been waiting for.

I made my way down the steps. After the first couple, which both squeaked as I planted my feet on them, I heard a voice call out, "Janie?"

I began to skip steps, but I only skipped three before I went tumbling down the staircase, ass over teakettle, just like in the cartoons. I landed on the linoleum of the first floor with a bang and rested there for a moment. The frame had definitely broken during the fall, and shards of wood and glass were stuck in my back.

The running water stopped.

"*Deb?*" the voice shouted.

By the time I heard the footsteps pounding the floor, heading in my direction, I was up and unlocking the deadbolt. The lock slid back, and my hand reached for the knob and pulled it down and swung the door wide open in one fluid motion. I was halfway down the block by the time I heard the shouts.

"Hey!" the man called out to me. "What the fuck are you doing?"

He didn't chase me, which was the only reason I didn't get caught. I ran track and cross country in high school—I still have the awards on a shelf in my room—but with pieces of wood and glass in my back, I was in no shape to outrun anyone.

When I got home, I rushed to the upstairs bathroom. I removed what was left of the photo and frame from underneath my clothes, lifted up my T-shirt, and faced my back toward the mirror. I saw some splinters and tiny pieces of glass along the small of my back, but there was only minor bleeding. I'm sure the majority of it was absorbed by my shirt.

"Stephen!" I heard my mom yell from downstairs. "That you?"

"Yeah, Mom!" I replied. "About to hop in the shower!"

I turned the faucet in the bath, and cold water came pouring out of the showerhead. It felt great against my back.

After my shower, I examined the frame and photo that I had rescued. The frame was broken nearly in half, so I tossed it in the waste basket. The photo was bent slightly down the middle, probably from when I fell down the steps. I turned the photo over and saw a note written in pencil. *Janie and Dan, Wildwood 2017*, it read. I turned the photo back around and tore along the crease and then through the entire photograph, separating Janie from "Dan," and I tossed Dan into the waste basket along with that tacky frame he must have gotten for her. I continued to stare into Janie's bright blue eyes. Or were they a light green? Her incredibly white teeth seemed to glisten as she smiled.

I was sure that that was Janie's room I had found. She lived eight blocks from me, but I had never met this woman before in my life. I couldn't allow that to stay the case. So every day I went for a run and made sure I passed her house twice. On the first day, I passed by her house at 6:47 in the morning and then again at 7:02 A.M., but I did not see her. On the second day, I passed by at 11:32 A.M. and then again at 11:47 A.M., but she was nowhere to be found. On the third day I passed at 12:06 P.M. and then again at 12:21 P.M., but there was still no sign of Janie. On the ninth day, I ran past the house at 5:05 P.M., and there she was, a black purse slung from her shoulder as she slammed the driver's side door of a silver Kia Sorento. I watched as she walked up the front steps of her house and went inside. I hurried my pace and ran past the house again that evening at 5:18, but she had not come back outside. The windows on the front of her house were all closed, along with the curtains. After I passed the house that second time, I doubled back and headed straight for the mailbox. I peeked inside and saw a stack of white and yellow envelopes. I pulled them out, careful not to get any sweat on them, and left the mailbox wide open. I made my way to the front door and used the knocker. After a few moments, the door swung open, and there in front of me stood the life-sized version of Janie. Well, yes, there stood Janie. The smile was missing from her face, and her frizzy blood red hair was now much straighter.

"Can I help you?" she asked me.

"Uh, well…" I struggled to speak, the words sticking to the inside of my mouth like peanut butter. "I believe these are yours," I said, handing her the stack of envelopes.

She furrowed her brow. "Thank you."

"Oh, no," I said, cracking a smile. "I was running by, and I saw these on the sidewalk, and the mailbox was wide open." I turned around and pointed toward the crime scene. "I didn't want these to blow away or something."

"Oh, thank you so much," she said, returning her friendly smile that I recognized so well from the photograph. "I really appreciate it."

Then the door began to close. I could feel she was gearing up to bid me farewell. I couldn't allow this moment to pass. I had to take the opportunity that was presented to me. So I slammed my hand against the door jam, closed my eyes, dipped my head, and dropped to one knee.

"Oh, God, are you all right?" she asked.

I nodded. "I'm fine. I'm fine. Just a little lightheaded." I used my other hand to wipe the thin layer of sweat from my forehead. "I pushed it too far during my run today. I have to keep reminding myself that I'm not a track star anymore." I let out a fake snicker.

"Do you need water?" She placed her hands under my arms and lifted me up. "Come on. Come inside." She led me into the kitchen. It was just on the other side of the staircase, closed off from the rest of the house by two swinging doors on either side of the room. She pulled a chair away from the round kitchen table. "Sit, sit."

I sat down, and she walked over to the fridge and pulled out a bottle of water and handed it to me. I took a long swig. "Thank you so much," I said to her. I hate drinking directly out of water bottles, but I didn't want to bring that up now.

She smiled.

"Do you often run around here?" she asked. "I've never seen you before."

"Well, I used to for a while, but then I stopped," I replied. "I just started up again. Hence the quick dehydration."

She chuckled.

"Have you been living here long?" I asked. "I haven't seen you around either."

"About a year and a half. I moved in with my

dad and sister. They've both been in town for a little over ten years."

I wanted to ask her who Dan was. Who's this Dan? Where's Dan now? I settled for a more appropriate question.

"Where are you originally from?" I asked. I took another swig from the waxy water bottle, nearly finishing it.

"Jersey City," she said. She moved over to the sink and took plates out of the drying rack and began stacking them in the cabinet above. "I used to work at a marketing firm in the city. Then I moved here after I got a job at one in Trenton."

Ugh, Trenton, I thought. Who's Dan?

"Who's Dan?" I asked.

"Huh?" She didn't look at me but continued stacking the plates in the cabinet. "How do you know Dan?"

"You had, you know, you mentioned him," I stammered. "Right? Didn't you say 'Dan' before?"

She was silent for a moment. "Oh, *Dad*, I had said." She laughed, and it hypnotized me. "I thought you were asking about my ex."

My heart rose to my throat. *Ex? Her ex?* I started to feel light and giddy. I must have been smiling, because when she turned back around and looked at me, her even face brightened, and she smiled and asked, "What's so funny?"

"No, nothing," I said. I tried my hardest to wipe the smirk off my face. I'm not sure if I was successful. "So you moved in with your dad and your sister, and Dan is just your ex?"

She grabbed some glassware out of the drying rack and placed them in another cabinet. It was beautiful glassware: short, crystal glasses with images of four separate roses etched around the outside. One glass was just small enough to fit into the pocket of my running shorts.

"Yes," she said. "Dad and Deb had lived here long before I moved in. Dan is..." The smile was now gone from her face. "Eh, forget it. He's not even worth the breath."

It had just then occurred to me that she and I were both alone in the house. I hadn't heard another sound since I knocked on the front door.

"Where are your dad and sister now?" I asked.

"Good question," she said. "Probably still at the store. They own Bart's Convenience on the Boulevard."

I nodded. I was familiar with the store but had never gone in before. I thought about acknowledging the business, but my heart was now racing, knowing that it was just the two of us—two good-looking singles—alone in the house.

"Hey, listen," I said, and she stopped what she was doing and leaned against the counter beside her. I placed both of my hands on the kitchen table. "Since you were so kind and didn't allow me to pass out on your porch…" She smiled. "Why don't you let me take you out for coffee or something?"

"Oh, no, that is not necessary," she replied, the smile not fading from her face.

"Come on. Nothing major. Just as a way of saying thank you."

Her smile grew, and she turned away.

"Now?" she asked, her back facing me as she turned the faucet next to the sink and slid her hands under the running water.

"Why not?" I answered. "I'll take a quick shower and be back in a half hour."

Janie agreed, and nine days after I saved that picture of her, we already had a date. I sprinted home and hurried through my shower and arrived back at her house twenty-eight minutes later.

The date was uneventful, but it had led to another, and then a few more. Within several weeks, I even felt comfortable enough to show her my collection, though I made sure not to tell her how these items were acquired. I led her to my bedroom, where I kept fossils and novelty pens and watches and all that displayed neatly on shelves. She probably thought I was into antiquing or some weird shit like that. I always kept the photo of her at the base of my nightstand so that it was never within sight, but it was still easily accessible when she wasn't around.

She looked at my trophies on a shelf between a Batman figurine I had found at a neighbor's house and a beer mug I had lifted from an Irish pub two towns over. The awards were organized in chronological order, from 2004 to 2007. I had seven trophies displayed on that shelf, which I hung using reinforced steel brackets. It was similar, kind of, to how Janie had set up her shelf above the dresser, but I didn't let her know that, because she still hadn't invited me up to her room yet.

"So you used to run track?" she asked.

"Yep," I said. "And cross country."

She nodded.

"Varsity," I added.

"Huh?"

"I lettered in track. I have the jacket and everything."

Next to the shelf was my walk-in closet packed

with boxes of little gems from my childhood. Well, most of the toys and collectables in those boxes were from *other* kids' childhoods, but it's all the same. In the far corner of my closet were a collection of coats. I reached toward to the back and pulled the green and black one off its hanger. I stepped out of the closet and handed it to Janie.

"Wow, this is a nice one!" she said, running her hand along the sleeves. She held it up and looked at the image of a lion—our school's mascot—on the back. She handed it back to me, and I folded it neatly in half and placed it on my bed.

I asked her what she thought of my collection.

"Cool stuff," she responded. "That jacket though—I have to say, that is really nice. I may have to borrow that from you when it starts to get cold out…" She winked at me and then giggled, and her freckles seemed to twinkle as she stared at my jacket. She grabbed her purse, which was sitting on the floor by her feet, and slung it over her shoulder. "I better get going."

"Okay," I said, "We'll do something tomorrow. Text me when you get home."

She nodded and gave me a peck on the lips. She slipped out of my bedroom and through the front door before I even had a chance to walk her out.

I took my old varsity jacket off my bed and returned it to its place in the closet, in between my new raincoat and a pea coat I had inherited from my great-grandfather.

I lay in bed and switched on the twenty-inch Sharp TV sitting on my dresser. The image always took a little while to appear, so I would often survey my room as I waited for the picture and sound. My desk was nice and neat, with my laptop exactly eight inches from each edge. The desk lamp was fixed in the far right corner. In the far left was my pencil sharpener and a collection of number two Ticonderogas in a commemorative mug. My bookshelf stood next to that, and all eighty-two books were aligned evenly on the six shelves. My dresser held a mirror in the center, and my little TV was off to the right, its picture still fuzzy. And in between my dresser and the closet was my shelf with the Batman figurine on the left, seven trophies in the middle, and a beer mug on the far right.

No, wait, I only saw six trophies this time. There was an empty space where my 2005 county trophy once stood. It wasn't a large space, but the trophies were no longer equidistant from each other, and it didn't take long for me to notice that. The statue depicting a fit man in full sprint was missing. It had been there just before, when I was showing them to Janie, but now it wasn't.

I looked on the floor to see if it had fallen, but there was nothing in the vicinity of the shelf. I got on my knees and peered under my bed, but it was clean. Not even a single dust bunny. Had someone stolen it?

Janie?

It must have been her, I supposed. But it couldn't have been.

I looked at my watch. It had been roughly twelve minutes since she noticed my trophies. All seven of them were there at the time. In those twelve minutes, no one had entered this room. I didn't see any other explanation.

I plopped my body onto my bed. I reached below my nightstand and removed the picture of Janie. She was just as beautiful as the first time I had seen this photograph. I gripped it so tightly between my thumb and index finger.

She stole from me. How could she steal from me? We've been friendly for more than five weeks, and she had stolen one of my prized possessions. She probably thought I wouldn't notice.

I felt a sense of betrayal that had never entered my being before. My heart was squirming. My mind was darting from one thought to another. My legs twitched, and my hands throbbed. I was restless and exhausted all at the same time.

I dropped her photograph on the bed. On my nightstand was a bottle of water Janie had left. I sat up in my bed and took a sip. It wasn't right. So I reached into the bottom drawer of my nightstand, pushed over a couple pairs of socks, and pulled out a short glass. I placed it on my nightstand and poured the water from the bottle into the glass, not stopping until the waterline reached the etchings of the four roses that surrounded the outside.

Philly to O'Hare

Darleena Trumple told me not to fly to Chicago. She told me that flying on an airplane is not enjoyable and that I'd have a much more pleasurable trip if I were to drive. But then I reminded Darleena Trumple just how much safer flying on an airplane is than driving in a car.

I said, "Last year, there were *zero* deaths in commercial passenger jets. And even overall, about ninety-six percent of airplane passengers on crashed flights survive anyway. However, more than *a million* people die in car accidents every year. There are around five million accidents each year alone. You tell me which mode of transportation is better then."

"Yes, but suppose you have to sit next to someone who twitches," she said to me. "Say you order a glass of orange juice, and Ms. Twitchy

Pants keeps spazzing in her seat, swings her arm, and knocks the O.J. all over your nice wool sweater."

I reminded her that I do not like orange juice, and my "nice wool sweater," which I never really cared for in the first place, has a large hole in it. So Ms. Twitchy Pants would be doing me a favor. Darleena didn't acknowledge that remark and instead left my home in a fuss; she dislikes when I insult gifts she's given me, but I told her that sweater was ugly when I first unwrapped it, so my distasteful comments should be no surprise to her now. She grabbed her long, burgundy raincoat off the coat rack next to the front door, nearly knocking it over, and stomped down the porch steps, leaving the door wide open.

She was my ride. So I was forced to take a taxi to the Philadelphia International Airport, which was probably for the better anyway. Darleena Trumple is a horrendous driver. She grips the wheel at four and eight o'clock and uses her right foot on the acceleration pedal and her left foot on the brake pedal. She also is clumsier than any "Ms. Twitchy Pants" she could ever fantasize about and spends more time riding the curb than the actual roadway. I suppose she did me a favor by abruptly departing that morning.

My taxicab smelled of cigarettes and nacho cheese, which may have been an improvement upon the odor emanating from the man sitting next to me on the plane. I was awarded the window seat but was unfortunate enough to have this pasty mess within breathing distance of me. He wore a pair of jeans that were so worn out they almost looked white, but they appropriately matched his decaying Coors Light T-shirt.

I cordially introduced myself, because that is the kind of thoughtful, open-minded man I am. "Timothy Haldenstein," I said, reaching out my right hand.

"I beg your pardon," he replied. Still, even with his eyebrow raised, he took my hand and shook, but when he lifted his arm, my nose was assaulted by the stench of sweat and decaying apples. *Macintosh Body Odor*, it might have read on the label of his deodorant stick.

"My name is Timothy Haldenstein," I told him, removing my hand from his grip and wiping it on my pant leg.

"Ah, I see." He scrubbed the bottom of his nose with the back of his index finger. "Tom… This is my wife, Denise." He pointed to the woman in the aisle seat.

I nodded before turning away to look out the window. We were still on the ground, and I saw a man in a fluorescent yellow vest waving large orange wands. I spent a few moments watching him swing his arms back and forth, but nothing seemed to change on the runway. When the plane began to move away from the jet bridge, I heard a yelp to my right. It was Denise.

Tom turned to me. "This is her first time flying," he said. "She's a bit nervous."

Denise was folded forward in her seat and had her head in her hands. She began rocking back and forth as the plane increased its speed as it approached the runway.

"You have nothing to worry about," I told the fetal woman. "The chances of this plane crashing are very low. In fact, you have a better chance of getting killed at O'Hare International Airport than on this plane."

Tom, who had been rubbing his hand on Denise's back, stopped and looked at me. "Thanks," he said.

"My pleasure." I smiled. "I am filled with statistics. For example, did you know Chicago had fewer homicides this past year than the year before, but it still has had a very large spike in homicide deaths in the past decade? Also, more than twenty percent of airplane passengers report being sick within a week after traveling. Bugs, viruses, and infections are passed so easily from passenger to passenger. So, see, Denise, you are more likely to get sick or die at your destination than end up a casualty of poor aviation choices."

Tom shook his head.

"It's true," I confirmed.

He stared at me. "Just be quiet, buddy," he said. "You're not helping at all."

I almost said, "I hardly ever find that to be true," but I decided to go back to looking out the window instead.

Only moments later, the plane rushed down the runway and lifted into the sky. We were among the clouds soon afterward, and I could not help but share with Tom and Denise all there was to know about clouds.

"We are flying through altocumulus clouds right now," I told the couple.

"Who cares?" said Tom.

"Well, don't *you*?" I asked. "This is a fascinating type of cloud. They mostly consist of cooled water droplets that are roughly fifteen degrees Fahrenheit. It's not going to start raining yet, but the weather will be changing soon."

"That's great," Tom said as he went back to running his hand up and down his wife's back. She continued to rock back and forth.

"Ah!" I shouted. "I almost forgot about the vomit bags." I reached into the pocket of the seat in front of me. Behind the wrinkled magazines, I found the crisp, flat paper bag utilized by passengers who like to vomit on the plane. I knew that Tom, being very confident and aloof, wouldn't need his, so I reached into the pocket in front of him and took that bag.

"What are you doing?" he questioned.

"I want the vomit bags," I told him.

"What for?" His voice was raised now.

"I use them for tons of stuff. Usually as lunch bags though." I reached across his lap and slid my hand into the pocket of the aisle seat. "Can I just…"

"Hold up!" Tom shouted. "That's my wife's. She might use it." He snatched the bag out of my hand when I pulled it out of the pocket. He seemed to glare at me, but I just turned back toward the window, two vomit bags neatly folded on my lap.

We were above the clouds now. I watched as

the aircraft raced above the giant cotton balls that appeared frozen beneath the sun. Within a split second, everything went hazy. We seemed to be flying through a cumulonimbus cloud now.

I reached across Tom's grotesquely large body and tapped his wife's shoulder. "Denise," I said, "don't be alarmed, but we are about to experience some turbulence."

"Leave her alone, pal," Tom demanded. "Don't stress her out even more with your nonsense."

Just then, the pilot came on the loudspeaker. "Uhhh, we will be experiencing some light turbulence," the pilot said in between crackles of the speaker. "It will be over shortly, but for now, I will be turning the fasten seatbelt sign back on. Thank you."

I smiled at Tom, but he didn't return it.

I removed a book from my backpack, which the flight attendant had forced me to stow away under the seat in front of me. That meant that someone else's carry-on bag must be underneath my seat, but I tried not to let it bother me. When I pulled out my mystery novel from the front pocket of the backpack and shoved the pack back under the seat, I noticed that Tom had reclined back in his space. This new position had caused him to become congested, I figured, because every thirty seconds or so he would snort, sucking mucus farther into his nostrils. After the eleventh time, I pulled my backpack onto my lap. In the side pocket, I kept a travel package of Kleenex tissues. I pulled it out and tapped Tom's belly.

"Please take one," I said to him.

He craned his neck to look at me. "What the hell is this?"

"They're tissues. You certainly need them at the moment. Please take as many as you need."

Instead of taking one, Tom snorted again. He reclined back in his seat and closed his eyes. Ten seconds later, he snorted once more. Seventeen seconds passed before he snorted again, then twenty-eight seconds, then six, then forty-eight. The snorts continued for several minutes before I spoke up again, the backpack still on my lap and tissue package in my hand.

"Please do not let this continue," I said politely. Tom didn't open his eyes or even move. He simply snorted. "I'm being polite," I told him.

He opened his left eye, peered at my lap, and grabbed the tissue package out of my hand and threw it down the aisle. Before he closed his eye again, he snorted.

I reached into the same side-pocket of my backpack and produced another travel package of Kleenex tissues. "I would greatly appreciate it if you would take one," I said to Tom, his eyes still closed. "Please don't throw these. This is my last package."

After several seconds, when Tom didn't move, I poked his belly with the tip of my index finger again. Denise, who had been seemingly incapacitated the entire flight, turned to me. Her eyes widened.

"I wouldn't do that if I were you," she said. Her hands were clenching the complimentary vomit bag. She still had not used it.

Perhaps I persisted too long, because Tom lurched forward, grasped my hand, and twisted it backward before I knew what was coming. The pain pulsed throughout my arm, and had I enough room, I probably would've fallen to the floor. Tom began to shout something at me, but I couldn't hear him over the ringing in my ears. I believe I was yelling too, but I wasn't crying like the newspapers claimed I had been. That, I am sure of.

I don't know how long it took the flight crew to respond, but soon enough they were on top of

Tom and his timid wife, who was once afraid of dying in a fiery crash but was now more concerned with getting trampled to death in her seat. They brought Tom somewhere, and Denise followed. All I know is that I have not seen or heard from him or his wife since, and I don't really care if I ever do again. Denise did leave her vomit bag on her seat when she grabbed her and her husband's carry-on bags, and I wasted no time snatching it up and sliding it into my backpack.

My arm has been in a sling for nearly three weeks, but now that I have returned home, it is finally starting to feel better.

Darleena Trumple had told me not to fly to Chicago. She told me that flying on an airplane was not enjoyable, but I don't like to let Darleena Trumple know when she is right, so I told her that I hurt my arm when I fell down while getting out of the taxicab that morning she stormed out of my house. Now, she feels terrible for making me take a taxi, and that's much better than letting her know she was right.

Junk Sale

"You know what I don't understand? How this *shit* could be worth *any*thing to somebody else." Darren threw down the cardboard box he was holding and used his shirt sleeve to wipe the sweat from his forehead after he spoke. The box, which contained scratched cassette tapes, baseball cards, broken picture frames, and He-Man toys, body-slammed the tiled floor with a heart-rattling crash.

"Darren!" his mom yelled. "Be careful with that stuff! And what did I say about cursing?!"

Darren left the box on the floor and repeatedly kicked it farther into the foyer of the house until it was sitting at his mother's feet. She stood by the open front door, dictating the direction the boxes went as if she were an air traffic controller for junk.

"Mom, you curse all the time," Darren said.

"That's because I have four boys," she replied. "If you have four boys when you grow up, I'll let you curse, too."

"Yeah, but that's not completely true, because once Francis turned eighteen, he was gone. And that was a long time ago, but you still curse."

"Fine. If you have even *three* boys, you can curse as much as you want." She picked up the box Darren had been carrying and peered inside. "And Francis didn't move out that long ago—he's only been gone a few years." She looked down at the rest of the boxes scattered by the front door. "Now be quiet and help your brothers bring up the rest of the boxes from the basement."

"That's some way to talk to your youngest child…"

Darren disappeared down the hall before his mother had a chance to respond to his sarcastic remark. Besides, she was focusing on more important matters anyway. The family was having their big spring yard sale. Just like every year, Mrs. Martin and her sons would lug boxes filled with old clothes, barely functioning toys, and terrible holiday gifts from the basement out to the curb, hoping some poor suckers would find their way to Brooks Lane and spend some pocket change on a bootleg

Beavis and Butthead T-shirt or a decade-old Guinness Book of World Records.

"This is the same junk we brought out last year, and the year before, and the year before that," Brent, the seventeen-year-old, complained as he passed his mom on his way out the front door. He was carrying a large cardboard box about the size of a mini-refrigerator.

"This stuff isn't *that* old," his mom snapped back.

"What're you talking about?" Brent shouted from the front yard. "All this stuff looks like it was bought at another yard sale! There's a freakin' Tamagotchi in here! This thing's been dead for, like, sixteen years! Who the hell is going to buy that?"

"Hey, Brent!" A barely audible voice came from the basement and bounced off the walls of the house, just making it far enough out the door so that Brent was able to hear it.

"What, Pete?" Brent called back as he re-entered the house.

Pete, the third Martin brother, was a year younger than Brent. His mom had called him her "happy surprise" when he was born. Two years later, Darren was born. He wasn't given any such epithet.

"Check out these CDs I found!" shouted Pete, still in the basement. "I think they're yours! Backstreet Boys, Britney Spears, the Pokémon Movie soundtrack!"

"Yup, they're definitely yours, Brent," Darren said as he meandered through the hallway with a plastic box. It was brimming with items the family hadn't seen since the last yard sale. Before Brent had a chance to react, Darren dropped the box on the floor, looked at his mom, and asked, "You sure you want me to bring this box out there with the rest of our stuff?"

"Of course," she answered. "Why not?"

"Well, let's take a look inside. First off, this is a stained pair of ripped jeans," Darren said, gripping the waist band of a pair of jeans with his thumb and index finger. A big coffee stain was visible right by the zippered fly, and at the base of each pant leg the fabric was fraying.

"We'll mark that down to a quarter," his mom said.

"What about this fish bowl?" Darren asked, pulling a glass bowl the size of a basketball out of the plastic box.

"What about it?"

"Well, aside from the fact we've never owned a fish, it's got a crack down the side." Darren tapped the three-inch-long crack with an index finger.

"So?" his mom questioned.

"So water's going to be leaking through it."

"Yeah, and…?"

"Um, do you know how fish work?"

Mrs. Martin rolled her eyes and turned to Pete, who stumbled into the foyer with a cardboard box filled with CDs and Disney VHS tapes.

"I think this is the last of it," he said.

"Are those VHS tapes?" Darren asked, pointing to Pete's box. When no one answered, Darren continued. "Those are VHS tapes! Mom, you're really trying to sell those?"

Darren's mom closed her eyes and let out a "Yes" with her sigh.

"Mom, no one owns a VCR anymore. What the hell are they going to do with a *Pocahontas* VHS and no way to watch it?"

His mom thought about ignoring him, but instead she said, "Darren, don't get so worked up. We go through this every year." She looked at her wristwatch. "We gotta hurry up. People are going to start coming soon."

"It's only seven o'clock," Brent said.

"Exactly. On the signs, I wrote that the yard sale is from 7:00 A.M. to noon."

"What?!" the three brothers shouted in unison.

"You put up signs?" asked Pete. "Where?"

"All over town. Main Street, Bulberry, McCarter Boulevard."

"McCarter Boulevard?!" This time it was just Brent.

"What's wrong with McCarter Boulevard?"

"Mom, that's where all the…" Brent paused, then whispered, "meth-heads live."

"Oh, please," she said. "Now hurry up and bring these boxes outside."

Brent, Pete, and Darren carried the rest of the boxes outside and placed them by the curb. Their mother had set up three fold-out tables on the sidewalk so that she could spread out all of their items neatly on top of them. She claimed it looked more presentable that way. Some items, like shoes and bigger toys, stayed on the ground.

"Where are the rest of the neighbors?" Darren asked. "Why aren't they waking up at the ass crack of dawn to drag some useless shit out to the curb?"

"Hey, what did I say about cursing?" Mrs. Martin shouted back. After a couple of breaths, she responded, "I don't know. I guess they're all out. The Millers, Warners, and Gebrans all went on some camping trip together. So that's half the street right there."

The boys helped their mom set everything up in their front yard, taking one item out of a box at a time and placing it in its annual location. Once the brothers finished organizing the site, they joined their mother on separate lawn chairs. They faced the yard sale, and the four of them watched as the visitors browsed through wrinkled coats, rubber dinosaurs, and a bin of universal remote controls.

After several cars of people arrived and disappeared in a matter of minutes, leaving Brooks Lane as lonely as it was a half hour before, Brent said, "I don't get it."

For a few seconds, his mom just sat in her lawn chair, deciding whether or not to bite. She bit. "You don't get what, Brent?" she asked.

"Why we do this every year," he replied. His mom opened her mouth to respond, but he continued. "All the people ever do is dig through the boxes, glance at the crap on the table, pick something up, ask how much it is—you say a quarter—

then they put it down and leave. It's not worth seven hours of our day—lugging everything outside, sitting around, then lugging everything back inside—for a lousy five bucks."

"Why don't we just donate this stuff to charity?" Pete offered.

"I've tried that," his mom said. "They never show up to take the stuff, and I'm not dragging it to them."

"Maybe we can just leave all of this junk out here, and if we're lucky, someone will take it," Darren said.

His mother was about to respond when her cell phone rang. She scooped it up, looked at the caller I.D., put the phone to her ear, and said, "What happened now?"

Mrs. Martin furrowed her brow. Then she shook her head, turned to her sons, and mouthed the word "Casey."

It was her shop.

She owned a healthy food store on Main Street and learned quickly that her employees only call her when something bad happens at the store. This time, the timid girl who placed the call informed her that the freezers stopped working, so all of the frozen food, including the sugar-free "ice cream" the boys loathed, were melting.

"*Dammit.* Okay… Okay, I'll be right there, Casey." Mrs. Martin hung up the phone.

"What happened now?" Brent asked his mom.

"Freezers broke again," she answered.

"Good," Darren said. "That's what that frozen shit deserves. Trying to call itself *ice cream*. It tastes like a wet Band-Aid dipped in blue cheese."

"That's oddly specific," Pete commented.

"It's called *imagination*, dumbass," Darren retorted.

Mrs. Martin ignored the repeated profanity and ran inside to grab her purse. When she came back outside, she said, "I'll be back in a few hours— probably around one or two o'clock. When I get back, I don't want to see any of this stuff out here. Not a single thing."

Brent, Pete, and Darren watched their mother hop into her white Nissan Sentra and take off down Brooks Lane. She made a hard left onto Valley Road and disappeared out of sight.

"Well, this blows," Darren said.

The road was empty. No one was outside playing or sitting on their porches. The neighborhood felt deserted.

"You guys wanna play catch?" Pete asked.

"No," Brent and Darren said without missing a beat.

"Shoot hoops?" Pete tried.

Another "No."

"So we're just going to sit here?"

"No," Brent answered. "I'm on my phone."

"Me too," said Darren, pulling an iPhone out of his pocket and mirroring Brent, who looked like The Thinker statue with a tiny rectangle in his paws.

The boys sat in silence for a few minutes before Pete broke it again.

"So you guys don't even want to talk at all?" Pete asked. He waited several seconds, but neither of his brothers responded. So he reached into his pocket, grabbed his cell phone, and sent a text message to Brent and Darren.

Anybody there?

Pete expected at least one of his brothers to lift his head from his phone and say something, but neither did. After a few seconds, Pete's phone buzzed. It was a message from Darren.

A little busy right now

"Oh, come on." Pete fell back into his seat. "You guys have got to be kidding me."

Pete was sixteen, but he felt the "rage of machines," as he called it, taking over his environment. Normally, stuff like that was inconspicuous to teenagers, but when technology is the only way to communicate with people who are sitting right in front of you, it's sort of hard not to notice a problem.

Pete ignored this disappointing interaction. His brothers were just messing with him anyway. He knew they were bitter because they had to wake up at six o'clock in the morning on their day off to bring boxes of stuff they don't want out to the curb. They've been helping their mom with this for years. Their dad used to help her, but when he died eight years ago, Brent, Pete, Darren, and their older brother Francis were happy to help out. Over the past few years, the brothers' mentalities have shifted. Hauling the same boxes up and down the stairs year after year is less enjoyable than it sounds, surprisingly. And not even the sentimental nature of this tradition was enough to keep the brothers from complaining.

The three of them sat in their front yard for several hours, waiting for the clock to strike noon.

At about a quarter to twelve, Darren sat up to start packing the boxes. He grabbed some items off one of the tables.

"Look at all of this *nice* stuff," he said. "A wireless router with a broken stand. A chipped vase. A pair of mismatched soccer cleats. An ugly picture frame with our family photo still in it. I'm surprised no one bought that…" He tossed a couple of the items into an empty box.

"Cut it out." Pete stood up to start collecting the belongings with his brother. Darren was holding the "ugly picture frame," and Pete snatched it out of his hand. It was a picture of the six of them from a family vacation more than a decade ago. They had gone down the shore. That was the year Pete forgot to wear sunscreen one day and burned so badly he couldn't lie down for a week. He had to sleep sitting straight up.

Pete slid the photo out of the frame and stuck it in his back pocket. Then he threw the frame into one of the cardboard boxes

"All right, Mom doesn't want to see this stuff here when she gets back," Pete reminded his brothers. "Let's start bringing some boxes back into the basement."

Brent looked up from his cell phone and

opened his mouth to protest, but the roaring of a truck's engine cut him off. Brent, Pete, and Darren turned to see a small white moving truck barreling down their street. It started to pass their house but stopped before the back of the truck completely passed the yard sale site. Two men jumped out of the front of the truck. Their faces were pale, and dark bags hung underneath their yellow-tinted eyes.

The shorter one with hair like steel wool spoke first. He looked at the three brothers and barked, "Hey! Pack this shit into the back of the truck."

The taller man unfastened a padlock and threw open the truck's roll-up door. As soon as the door opened, the boys saw decrepit furniture and trash littered throughout the trailer, and they were smacked with a stench that made wet Band-Aid and blue cheese seem like freshly baked cookies and piping hot coffee.

Brent, Pete, and Darren didn't move.

"Well, hurry the fuck up, boys," the taller one said. "We ain't got much time."

That broke the brothers' trance, and they started piling the boxes, one at a time, into the back of the truck. The two strangers stood close by and watched them, making sure the boys got every-thing—including the three fold-out tables—into the back of the dilapidated truck.

After Pete threw the last box into the back of the truck, one of the Martin family's neighbors turned onto Brooks Lane. The blue sedan of the Colers pulled into their driveway two houses down.

"Shit," the tall stranger said. "Hurry up an' get that thing closed."

The shorter one threw down the door on the back of the truck, and the bang echoed throughout the neighborhood. Both men hopped into the front seats, and the truck took off.

The boys stood at the curb for a few moments, watching the white truck disappear down an adjacent street. Darren was the one to break the silence.

"What the fuck was that?" he blurted out.

Neither brother responded. For a few more seconds, Brent and Pete stood still.

"I guess that's it, right?" Brent said, scratching the back of his head. "It's not like we have anything to bring back inside now."

Pete looked around. Their front lawn was empty. No more old clothes. No more used toys or out-of-date technology. Those two unwelcomed visitors even took the lawn chairs the brothers and their mother had been sitting in.

Brent started toward the house, and his brothers followed.

"Damn," Darren said, "I guess it was a good thing Mom put a sign up on McCarter Boulevard… Huh."

Don't Hire Me

I don't want this job.

It's my fault for agreeing to the interview. I don't know what I was thinking. Wait, yes I do—I was thinking, *I want to eat.*

But I'd eat regardless, even without this job. I live with my parents. They rarely threaten to let me starve anymore.

I guess when you graduate from college and don't get hired immediately after you take off your cap and gown, you get anxious. It's unfounded and irrational, but you're anxious nonetheless.

So here I am, five months after graduation, waiting for Part Two of my interview for a customer relations position. I'm in a small conference room where the rectangular table governs most of the space. The room is so tight, in fact, that if I move my leather office chair back any farther, I'll hit the yellow wall behind me. I'm sure at one point these four walls were white, but now they're stained like the flaxen chompers of a veteran smoker.

Everything in this room is garbage, actually. My chair has seen the asses of so many pretentious business slobs that I'm surprised it's not a golden toilet. What else would they do with all of that invaluable bull shit?

Now that I look around, I'm noticing that most of these chairs are different. There are about a dozen chairs around the table and five different styles of them, some brown with square headrests, others black with rounded backrests. But all are discolored and worn, and some—like mine—are ripped and frayed around the leather-bound armrests.

There is one inspirational poster hanging on each of the four walls—"BELIEVE" made into an acronym and crap like that—and each frame is layered with dust.

In one corner, there's a stool that blends in with the walls, and on the stool is a brown microwave— the same type of microwave my grandparents probably owned when they first got married. The door of the appliance is wide open, and there is a coffee mug inside. If I had to guess, I'd say there is probably someone's stale coffee staining the inside of that mug right now.

High on the wall above the microwave is an analog clock. Well, *most* of a clock. The numbers from three to six are missing, like a bear took a bite out of the bottom-right end of the clock. Instead, there is a piece of printer paper taped to the wall behind that edge of the clock. The hours of three, four, five, and six are written on an outward curve in magic marker.

You are interviewing a potentially new employee, and this is the room you choose to make the first impression?

Actually, the first impression was made when I couldn't even find this place. It's a warehouse, among many, many other identical warehouses, on Springer Street in Edison. If it weren't for the bold black numbers on the side of the building, I might never have known that this was Vacation Trading Corp., 468 Springer Street, Edison, New Jersey.

The second impression was made when I entered the warehouse, expecting to be greeted with the smiling face of a preppy secretary. Instead, I was met with the scowling glare of an elderly security guard.

"Name?" he asked.

"Thomas Kirby," I answered.

"Have a seat," he said. "They'll call you when they're ready."

He pointed to three rolling office chairs aligned against the far wall. I sat in the only unstained one.

I was twenty minutes early for my interview, but I still sat there for more than half an hour, watching warehouse workers yell and load electronic equipment into small trucks. To my left was the office part of the building. The wall separating the warehouse from the office wasn't made of plaster and wooden beams; it was made of plywood. Just plywood. And I still have no idea how it was being held up. There was a large rectangular hole in place of a door, and from that hole emerged a hefty man in a dark green Polo and faded blue work pants.

"Thomas Kirby?" he said, looking at me.

"Yes," I said.

"Right this way."

He led me through a break room with a few small tables and a couple vending machines. He opened the door of the room next to it and said, "Have a seat anywhere you like. Someone will be right with you."

Comforting, I thought. I came in as an interviewee but am treated like a patient. Another impression was made at that moment.

I found the seat closest to the door and waited for the doctor. After a few minutes, a man with thin rectangular glasses, curly gray hair, and a dark red Polo came in, and I stood up to greet him. The top button of his shirt was undone, and his equally curly gray chest hairs were reaching out of the opening like the legs of a desperate spider.

Impression number four.

"Thomas," he said, gripping my hand like a stress ball. "Gregg Ulipsee. Nice to meet you."

"Nice to meet you," I replied.

We both sat down, and he pulled a sheet of paper out of his manila folder: my résumé. I worked at a diner throughout college and graduated magna cum laude last spring. Anything more than that was just filler bull shit put in to make my résumé look "healthy." That didn't stop this guy from saying, "Very impressive, Thomas."

"Thank you," I replied.

"What was your favorite course in college?" he asked.

"I'd have to say the biology course I took last year about diseases. We studied different viruses, infections, and sicknesses."

"Interesting." He paused. "It says here you studied English… Tell me about that."

"Sure," I said. "I took a number of literature and writing courses. We read anything from sixteenth century poetry to modern works. And I wrote a lot of essays."

He didn't react to my shoddy answer. His glasses sat on the tip of his nose. I was afraid they might fall off. But Interviewer Gregg didn't move a muscle. Only his eyes seemed to twitch. They just moved from my résumé to me and back to my résumé.

"Tell me about a time you were put under a lot of pressure at work and how you resolved that situation," he requested.

"One day, we were running an all-you-can-eat promotion on our cheeseburger sliders and fries," I told him. "Nearly every one of the people I served ordered them. It got very busy and very complicated, so after a little while, I started telling my tables that we ran out of cheeseburger sliders."

"Okay…"

"It started to calm down after that. So I'd say I certainly resolved that situation."

Gregg squinted and finally pushed the glasses

close to his face, pressing his fingers against the lenses as he did so. His gaze was fixed on me. Then he sat up in his chair and asked, "But was the restaurant really out of cheeseburger sliders?"

"No," I answered.

"Then didn't your guests see that people at the other tables were getting cheeseburger sliders after you said you were out of them?"

"Some did."

He pinched his earlobe. "Well, what did you tell them?"

"I pretended to go in the kitchen to ask the cooks what the deal was, and then I ignored those guests until the end of their meals."

Gregg scratched the bottom of his chin and nodded. "Very good," he said, but I was convinced he didn't know how else to respond. Couldn't he tell I don't want this job? I don't think I could have made that any clearer if I shouted "Don't hire me!" from a megaphone.

Gregg stood up and extended his hand. "It was nice meeting you, Mr. Kirby," he said. "Your second interviewer will be right with you."

I stood up and shook his hand. When he walked out, I plopped back into my seat.

I've been waiting here for exactly forty-eight

minutes now. I haven't seen a soul since Gregg Ulipsee rushed out of the room. I'm sick of playing on my phone. I can't stare at these sad walls anymore. I wonder if they forgot about me. Every few minutes, I lie back in my chair and gaze at the ceiling. The panels are scratched and broken, and there are even two that are completely missing, exposing the wiring and insulation—probably asbestos—that hang above.

What the hell do they do in here?

I look at the clock above the microwave. Fifty-two minutes. I have been alone in this room for fifty-two minutes, and no one else has come in to interview me. Like I said, I don't even want this job. Why am I waiting? I can either go get someone's attention or walk out of the building and forget about this experience.

It's about lunch time, so there has to be at least one person in the break room. I can hear the chatter outside the door.

"Marcus," a young male's voice says, "I understand you haven't received your paycheck yet, but my dad *just* mailed them out yesterday. Check your mail when you get home today."

"It's two days late, Dave," an older man's voice responds.

"I know, I know," the first voice says. "But it's coming. Don't worry."

Their voices trail off down the hall, and I look back at the clock. I have been in this room, by myself, for fifty-six minutes. I'll stick it out for four more. If no one comes, I'll leave.

I hear a stomping down the hall. Maybe this is my interviewer rushing to meet me. I anticipate another hairy, hefty man barging in, sweating profusely through the pits of his tattered Polo. But the footsteps pass the door and run out of earshot farther down the other side of the hall. I listen for more sounds. Voices, footsteps. Something. But I don't hear anything. I look at the clock, and it tells me I'm an idiot. I've been here for fifty-eight minutes, waiting to interview for a job I don't want at a place whose employees don't care.

Then the doorknob rattles, and a woman with dark brown hair and all-black attire walks into the room. She uses her right hand to adjust the thick-rimmed glasses on her nose and then extends it out toward me.

"I am so, *so* sorry," she says to me. "Mr. Ulipsee was supposed to tell me when to come in, but his attention was directed elsewhere, and he never did."

I stood up and shook her hand.

"I had no idea if you were even here yet," she says.

"It's no problem," I say.

"I'm so, so sorry," she says again.

This time I don't respond.

"Please, sit down. I'll make this interview as painless as possible," she says with a smile.

I smile back. Like an idiot.

She's not looking at me anyway. She's inspecting a piece of paper that I'm sure is my résumé.

While her eyes are still focused on the document in her hands, she says, "So I'm sure you know all the details about the position."

"Yes," I reply, even though she wasn't asking a question.

"Your main duty will be taking phone calls, which you'll be doing all day. I'm not sure if Mr. Ulipsee told you already, but Mondays through Thursdays you'll be working from 9:00 A.M. until seven o'clock in the evening. Fridays are nice half-days, from 9:00 A.M. to 2:00 P.M. Then every Saturday we are closed. But I will need you to work three or four Sundays a month."

"Oh, I thought the job posting stated I'd be

working one Sunday every three or four weeks."

"No, that's not right," she says, finally making eye contact with me. "New customer relations representatives always work three or four Sundays a month."

"So basically every Sunday."

"Basically." She chuckles. "But eventually you'll be down to one or two a month."

"Great," I say, glancing back up at the half-eaten clock.

"Halloween is coming up in a couple weeks," she says.

"Yes, it is."

"Halloween to the end of January is our busiest period. We run overtime hours. So Monday through Thursday you'll be here until around eight o'clock, and I'll need you to work every Sunday."

"Of course," I say.

"You'll be compensated for overtime, obviously."

"Now, what exactly does the position pay?"

"We'll get into that once you're hired. But right now I think it's important to warn you that you will be taking phone calls nonstop from the time you come in each morning until the time you leave every evening."

"Well, except for when I'm on break, right?"

"Nonstop," she reiterates. She looks back down at my résumé, turns it over to look at its blank back, and then she glares back at me. "We're a highly accredited company with a great retention rate. We compensate well, and there's room to move up."

Yeah, if your dad is the one mailing the paychecks, I want to say.

"We'd love for you to start this Monday," she says. "Would you be interested in working for us?"

I break eye contact with her and look back at the clock in the corner of the room one last time. How can I answer this question? There are so many different ways to say no. So I look at her again, interlock my fingers like I'm praying, bang them on the table in front of me, and proclaim, "Of course!" I even smile as I say it, and she smiles back.

Then she extends her hand, and we shake.

What the fuck is wrong with me?

Wife Swap

My wife, Janet, tossed a couple dirty porcelain plates into the kitchen sink. She was careful enough so that they wouldn't break but just aggressive enough so the deafening crash would get my attention. The plates were slick with the milky residue of her "famous homemade" pancakes, so they made more of a splash than a crash. I still pretended I didn't hear it. I was sitting at the kitchen table enjoying a bowl of Froot Loops and reading the newspaper. I needed something edible to erase the flavor of that dough and sand I had just consumed.

When I didn't respond to the noise, Janet asked, "What are you doing today?"

"Taking Jack to the park," I replied.

Janet pushed her stale blond hair out of her eyes and muttered something under her breath. I ignored her again and poured myself a second bowl of cereal.

"Jeez, Kenny," she said. "If you're going to eat like an animal, you could at least wash your friggin' bowl when you're done."

"You got it, dear."

Janet sighed and began to wash the plates, not saying another word.

My cell phone was lying next to my cereal bowl when it went off. The blasting, generic ringtone so close to my face made me jump. It was my buddy, Riley, calling. We were supposed to meet up at the park this morning for a "playdate" for our two-year-olds, but, really, it was a playdate for us. We've been close ever since we started teaching at Hillsborough Middle School almost ten years ago. We're in the same "pod," as we call it. I teach reading and writing; he teaches math, and our classrooms are side-by-side. So we see a lot of each other throughout the day.

Janet asked me who was calling so early in the morning, but I didn't respond. I scooped my phone off the kitchen table and answered it. I was choking on a mouthful of sugary cereal, but if I didn't answer, he wouldn't stop calling.

"You ready for our first playdate of the

summer, asshole?" Riley said on the other end of the line.

"Of course, shithead!" I replied, spitting a bit of milk onto the kitchen table.

"Ugh, Riley," Janet mumbled, rolling her eyes.

"I'm finishing up breakfast now, so I'll head out in ten minutes," I told Riley.

"All right, sounds good," he said. "See ya in a few."

I hung up the phone and went back to my Froot Loops. Janet was still washing the plates. When I finished my cereal, I walked the bowl over to the sink.

"You know," I said to Janet, "since you're already washing dishes…"

"Just give it to me," she said, and I threw the bowl into the sink and ran into the living room.

Our baby, Jack, was sitting on the couch watching *Sesame Street* or *The Muppets* or some other children's show with those same creepy puppets. I'm not a fan of these programs—what parent is?—but if it keeps my kid from screaming and crying, I'll keep it on twenty-four seven.

Riley hasn't had that same luck with his little girl Brittney, who's a couple months younger than Jack. She'll scream and cry no matter what you put on the TV. I told him she'll grow into it eventually. After all, I became a father two months before him—I should know.

I turned the television off, and Jack let out a window-shaking baby whine. Before he could form tears, I said, "Come on, Jack. We're going to the park!" He stopped screaming and turned his head, locking eyes with me. If there's one thing my kid loves more than creepy TV puppets, it's the lake at Ann Van Middlesworth Park, which he knows as simply "the park."

I handed Jack his sippy cup of water, picked him up, strapped him into his stroller, and we were off.

Ann Van was about half a mile from my house, maybe even closer. You can hear the kids at Ann Van's skate park from my backyard. Riley lives only a few houses down from the park's entrance, so I couldn't get there without passing the diarrhea green paneling of his colonial.

As I got closer to his house, I saw him struggling to strap Brittney into the stroller. She kicked and screamed, but after a little while, Riley finally reached into a pocket at the base of the stroller, revealed a bright orange pacifier, and stuck it in his daughter's mouth. In a few seconds, she was silent and started fluttering her eyes until they closed completely.

I stopped at the end of Riley's driveway. "All set?" I asked him.

"Let's go," he said, and we headed to the park together, just two dads pushing strollers. Last year, I tried talking him into buying a tandem stroller for Jack and Brittney, but his wife, Bonnie, wasn't a fan of the idea, arguing that it's a waste of money. What she doesn't realize is that I watch *Shark Tank* pretty religiously, so I know a good investment when I see one. And that is a phenomenal one.

When we got to the park, we sat our kids down in the woodchips by the swings and dumped a pile of action figures, dolls, and plastic toy shovels next to them—you know, standard park paraphernalia. We found a ledge a few feet away, took a seat, and watched them play.

Riley hadn't said anything since we greeted each other at his driveway about fifteen minutes earlier, so I asked, "How's your summer going so far?"

"It's only the first day," he answered. He cracked a smile, but his eyes seemed to get damp as he looked at me.

"Yeah, I know," I said. I didn't wait for a

response and asked, "How's Bonnie doing?"

"Kenny…" he said, looking down at his hands. They were interlocked and strung over his bent knees like tied shoes over a telephone wire. He shook his head and then looked back at me. "How do you put a hit out on someone?"

He asked me that as casually as he'd ask how one goes about taking out a mortgage. He broke eye contact with me and looked down at the ground between his legs. He separated his hands and started picking at some gunk on the side of one of his dirty white Nikes. His short, dark brown hair bounced in the wind. When I didn't respond, he continued.

"Seriously," he said. "How do you put a hit out on someone?"

"On Bonnie?" I asked, raising my voice a notch too loud.

"No!" he shouted. "On another man."

"What are you talking about, Riley?"

"Well, I don't want to, like, kill him. I just want him roughed up a bit, at least. You know, a couple scrapes and bruises, maybe a black eye. That type of stuff."

"Riley, start from the beginning," I demanded. "I have no clue what you're talking about."

"Bonnie's having an affair," he said, lifting his head and making eye contact with me again.

"Jeez… How do you know?"

"It's so fucking obvious. She's over this guy's house every day. She's going to see him now."

"Who?"

"That foreigner down the block. They—"

"Gianluigi?"

"No." He shook his head. "Ted."

"Ted's not a foreigner," I said. "I think he's from Mississippi. Plus, he's, like, seventy years old."

"Jesus, Kenny, would you just listen to me?" Riley shouted.

"Sorry, go ahead."

Riley waited a couple seconds before speaking again. "Well, that's basically it." He picked up a stone that was lying by his feet and tossed it a couple inches in the air and then caught it. Without getting up from the ledge we were sitting on, Riley swung his body around on his rear end and fired the stone into the manmade lake behind us. He stayed in that position, hunched over and glaring out over the lake, so I turned around too. Then he added, "I want to put a hit out on this guy. Do you know anyone who would kick his ass?"

"You mean, do I know anyone who's into beating old people?"

"I'm serious, Kenny. This guy's ruining a family."

I chuckled. I felt sorry for him—I really did—but I had to focus on defusing this bomb before our senior citizen neighbor got assaulted.

"How is he the one who's ruining your family?" I asked. Riley didn't answer right away, so I kept talking. "The first thing you need to do is look at this objectively and ask yourself if your family unit was stable up until he and your wife became friendly."

"Yes, it definitely was," Riley said. "They just started hanging out a few weeks ago, and that's when Bonnie and I started having stupid little squabbles all the time."

"Seriously?"

"What?" Riley asked, curling his upper lip.

"You guys have been fighting for years. This isn't new!" I threw my head back and laughed. "Last year, you boycotted an entire season of *A Game of Thrones* because Bonnie watched one episode without you. The year before that, she banned you from ever going back to the Red Lobster because you were 'overly friendly' with one of the waitresses."

"That's out of context."

"You guys have stupid little squabbles all the time, Riley. And you're rubbing off on Brittney." I took a deep breath. "Janet and I are the same. I don't mean to undermine your marriage. But I guess most couples go through shit like that. I wouldn't worry about it if I were you." I put my hand on his shoulder. Then, realizing this was real life and not an episode of *Full House*, I pulled it away.

"I don't know, man," he said, scratching his shoulder.

"Plus," I added, "even Janet has become good friends with Ted recently. She goes over to his house; he comes over to ours. He's a really friendly guy, Riley. He's a Vietnam vet! I'm telling you— you have nothing to worry about."

Riley was back to staring at his sneakers. He shook his head, unconvinced.

"But if you're still concerned about this," I said, "you need to tell Bonnie. I'm here to listen, but, ultimately, the only way to truly resolve this issue is for you to communicate with your wife."

"Yeah," Riley mumbled, taking a deep breath after his lengthy response. Then he topped it off with, "I don't know."

I turned around and looked over at our kids. They were digging holes with the toy shovels. Guess what they were burying… Their shoes. About a dozen dolls lay right in front of them, but they were burying their shoes.

I stood up. "All right, that's enough, guys," I said to the kids. "It's time to go." Both Jack and Brittney turned their heads and looked at me. Jack had the butt end of a little red shovel sticking out of his mouth. "It's time to go home," I repeated.

"No!" Brittney shouted. Her long, curly brown hair twisted around as she shook her head with vigor. With that, Riley stood up, too.

"Yes, honey," he said. "We have to get you cleaned up. You look like a midget grave robber."

Brittney tried not to smile at that. She was only two years old and obviously didn't understand what he meant, but Riley's voice got a little higher-pitched whenever he joked around, and you couldn't help but laugh.

We put our babies back into their separate strollers and headed to our homes.

As we approached Riley's house, he said, "Listen, Kenny, I really appreciate you trying to ease my mind about Bonnie."

"Of course, man," I said.

"I mean, I'm still going to keep obsessing about it, but I appreciate the effort."

We chuckled and said goodbye.

Jack began to stir in his seat as I pushed him up our driveway.

"We're here, Jack," I said, taking him out of the stroller and letting him run through the front door of our house.

I folded the stroller up and leaned it against the house next to the front door. When I walked into the kitchen, I saw Janet and Ted sitting next to each other at the kitchen table.

Ted, the seventy-year-old Vietnam vet, had a steaming cup of coffee in front of him. He was wearing a baby blue button-down shirt with a gray sweater vest over it, even though it was eighty-four degrees outside. His wiry white hair was gelled back, and it even looked like he was cleanly shaven.

"Hey, Ted, how's it going?" I asked. "I thought you were hanging out with Bonnie today."

"Oh, no," he said. "Not today. I decided to come over here and spend some time with your lovely wife." He smiled and looked at Janet.

"Ah, okay, that's nice," I said. "Now did you see where Jack went? We have to give him a bath."

Janet and Ted didn't respond. They both stared

at me, then looked at each other. I started getting irritated with their silence. We had a rogue two-year-old loose in the house.

"Did you see where he went?" I repeated.

Janet and Ted both looked at me, then back at each other again.

Before I could voice my frustration, Ted opened his mouth to speak, but Janet put her hand on his arm and said, "No, it should come from me."

I was going to say something when Janet started to laugh. "You know," she said, "I really have no idea how to begin here."

"Just tell him," Ted said, taking my wife's hand into his.

Janet looked down at their interlocking fingers and then back up at me.

"Kenny," she said, "there is something that Ted and I need to tell you…" Her voice trailed off.

At that moment, my cell phone rang. I took it out of my pocket and looked at the caller I.D.

It was Riley. I knew he wouldn't stop calling if I didn't pick up, so I put the phone to my ear and said, "Listen, Riley, this isn't really a good time."

"No, that's fine," Riley responded. "I just wanted to thank you for your advice. Bonnie was home when I got back, and I told her what was bothering me. She assured me that there was never anything going on between Ted and her, and she said she doesn't plan on visiting him ever again anyway." Riley paused, but I didn't say anything, so he continued. "It turns out that Ted is actually having an affair with someone else's wife. They are actually going to get together, too." He chuckled, and using his comically higher-pitched voice, he said, "Man, am I glad I'm not that poor schmuck."

With the phone pressed against my ear as I stared at my wife and Ted's frowning faces, I couldn't help but let out a sharp snort. Fucking Riley cracks me up.

Grocery Knight

You are a guy, and like your female counterparts, you too were told the stories of knights in shining armor who stormed into the dungeons and saved the beautiful princesses, the damsels in distress, as it were. You too were under the impression that when you meet a woman—one so enthralling that you always fantasize about her, whether you're in the shower or waiting for your train to arrive—you would become the knight in shining armor, the stoic prince, and she would become the damsel in distress, the princess who could finally find happiness.

So that's how you felt when you met Briana.

Of course, she was the new cashier at the local ShopRite; you worked part-time in the bakery for the past two years. If you were the new one in the "tale," it'd be much harder for you to be her hero.

Your station in the bakery gave you a clear view of her register, number six. She wore her blond hair in a ponytail and always draped it over her shoulder. Her baby blue blouse shined underneath her thin red ShopRite vest. When she looked your way, you could see the darkness of her brown eyes, like chocolate coins, and you also could see the touch of rosiness in the summits of her cheeks.

She smiled whenever she spoke, even when it was just a few words to Joe, the bagboy at register six. Joe stood about five feet tall, a couple inches shorter than Briana, and he had a terrible case of what employees called "pizza face." In other words, it would be impossible to play connect the dots with Joe's facial acne without coloring in his entire face. It didn't seem to faze Briana, however. He might say something to her, and she would lean back and laugh, touching his arm to keep her balance. If someone who looked like that could make her laugh, you knew she must have a kind, charming spirit.

You spent hours wondering how you could get her attention. You thought about starting a band, but then you'd have to learn an instrument, and you weren't sure that your *Guitar Hero* skills would transfer. What you needed was a haircut, you thought. That frizzy brown mop wasn't doing you or your shower drain any favors. Maybe you could even bleach it, show how wild you can truly be. But that would cost money you weren't willing to get rid of just yet. You needed to *do* something— something that would simultaneously show her you were fun, spontaneous, *and* hot. You should start a fire, you considered. But it didn't take you long to rule out that idea.

As you watched her ring up a cartful of some woman's cold cuts and Lunchables, your stomach started to growl. You were so entranced by her that you almost missed your lunch break.

You were alone in the breakroom, eating a peanut butter and jelly sandwich at a table meant for four, when she tiptoed in on that first day. She smiled at you, and those sunken, dark brown eyes of hers seemed to brighten. She pulled out the seat across from you—the one you had accidentally spilled water on earlier—and before she could place her brown paper lunch bag on the table, you, with your chest puffed out, said, "Don't sit there. It's wet." And you saved her black work pants from being ruined.

She had said, "Oh, thank you," but you didn't

reply. Instead, you handed her the napkin you used to wipe the jelly from the corner of your mouth, and she used it to dry her seat.

When she sat down, she pulled the hair tie out of her pony tail and retied it into a bun. She caught you staring and chuckled. You thought about saying something to break the awkward silence, but you weren't sure what a knight would say. You knew a knight had to prove himself, demonstrate how he is worthy of courting a princess. So you decided to show her how cool you were, and what's cooler than a knight's stead?

"My new car has a rearview camera," you told her.

The corner of her lip twitched.

"And it's a push-button start," you added.

"That's cool," she said, reaching into her lunch bag and revealing a square wrapped in tinfoil.

Nailed it, you thought as you smiled and took another bite of your PB & J.

"That sandwich must be good," she said.

"Huh?" you replied, eyes wide and crumbs freefalling from your mouth.

"You had a big smile on your face. So I said that sandwich must be good." She chuckled.

"Oh… Yeah, it is."

Rolland, a full-time stock clerk, entered the breakroom. He stood six and a half feet tall, nine inches taller than you. He had unreasonably black hair, to the point that it looked like he styled it with a glob of tar every morning. His jaw was square, and his facial hair was in a perpetual state of scruff. The only contrast was the color of his bright blue eyes that held a ring of white.

Briana's back was facing the door, so while Rolland ogled her from behind, she had no idea. He pulled out the chair next to her and sat down. She turned to him and smiled.

"So how's your first day going so far?" Rolland asked her.

Dammit, you thought. *How did I not think to ask that?*

"It's going well," she said. She had unraveled the ham and cheese sandwich from the foil and now was nearly finished with it.

"Briana, is it?" Rolland asked.

"Yes," she answered after she swallowed another bite.

"Great to finally meet you."

Rolland stuck out one of his large hands, and they shook. From that moment, you knew he was the villain. The black knight.

He grinned at you.

"Mike," he said. "How's the bakery going?"

"Fine," you replied.

"No more mishaps?" he asked.

You didn't answer. You shoved the rest of the sandwich into your mouth as you glared at Rolland.

Rolland broke eye contact, turning to Briana to say, "So last month, this kid isn't paying attention when he's making the bagels. He adds *way* too much salt—like, a few cups' worth—and the bakery smells like the Atlantic Ocean for a week straight." Rolland reached into the plastic shopping bag he called a lunch box, pulled out a slice of pizza, and took a bite. The sauce and mozzarella looked like they were welded together. The pizza was probably made weeks ago and left forgotten in the back of a refrigerator.

While still chewing on the leftover pizza, Rolland opened his mouth and said, "Guess what our bagel sales were that week."

Briana shrugged.

"Twelve dollars." He snickered. "And that's including all the ones that were returned for a refund."

Briana broke a smile and looked at you, but your lips didn't move. Your face might've been turning red, so you took a swig from your water bottle.

How do you beat a villain? Retaliate. Tell Briana about the time… about the time Rolland…

Jeez, you thought, *has Rolland never messed up?*

Not as long as you've worked with him.

You got out of your seat, tossed your scraps into the garbage can, and walked out of the breakroom. As you were walking through produce, you realized that you forgot to say "See ya" to Briana before you stormed out. You shrugged and kept on walking toward the bakery.

Your shift ended at the same time Briana's did that night. You knew that because you peaked at the schedule after your break.

When you walked out of the store, you saw her. She was sitting on the rickety aluminum chair of a discount patio dining set that ShopRite was trying to pawn off on someone who buys furniture from a grocery store.

Briana heard the automatic doors open as you passed through them, and she turned to look. She smiled and said, "Hey, Mike."

"Hey, Briana," you replied. "What are you doing hanging out here?"

"Waiting for my mom to come pick me up," she said. "She's got my car today while hers is in the shop."

"She gonna be long?" you asked.

"Probably. She's coming from work, which is about forty-five, fifty minutes away."

"Huh." You pulled your car keys out of your pocket and thought about waiting with Briana until her mom showed up. But a new episode of *Modern Family* was about to air, and you wanted to get home before it did. So you looked back down at her and said, "That sucks. See you tomorrow." Then you headed toward your car in the lot.

As you grabbed the handle of the driver's side door, you realized what a mistake you had made. So you shoved your keys into your pocket and hurried back to the discount patio set. You were about to call Briana's name when you saw her stand up from the rickety chair and start walking toward the opposite side of the parking lot. She was walking with someone—someone tall—but it was difficult to see who it was in the darkness. Then his face turned your way, and you saw the prominent scruff and trenchant white eyes.

Grocery Knight

~   *   ~

Your mind reverted back to that of the knight, or *a* knight—one who knows that he must save his darling dearest, because she is incapable of saving herself. That's what the stories suggest. A woman gets herself into trouble, and a brave man is destined to save her. As Rolland is the villain, and Briana is his victim, you know that she must be saved.

The next day at work, you knew her break was at noon, so you took yours at the same time. You sat in the same seat as you did the day before and began unpacking your peanut butter and jelly sandwich made by your mom. There might've been a loving note in there too, but she stopped doing that when you turned twenty-one.

Briana strolled in a few minutes after noon, her hand strangling a brown paper bag. She sat down across from you without making eye contact.

So you asked, "How's your second day going so far?" wondering if this was the pattern you wanted to follow the rest of your life—asking Briana how each day of work was going. *How's your three hundred sixty-fifth day going so far?*

How's your nine hundred forty-fourth day going so far?

Briana finally looked at you after she took Tupperware stuffed with strawberries and grapes out of her lunch bag. She sighed and said, "Not that great."

You thought about asking why, but your mom's sandwich was beckoning for another bite. That didn't stop her from telling you anyway.

"Are Sundays always so miserable?" she asked you.

You shrugged. You would've asked, "What the hell are you talking about?" but your mouth was being controlled by the heavy peanut butter that forced it to remain shut.

"I don't know what it is," she continued, "but every other customer has an issue—people trying to use expired coupons, others changing price tags thinking we wouldn't notice. And why does everyone pay with checks on Sundays? What is that?"

You thought of something funny Rolland had said about working Sundays.

"Sunday's when the mental institutions allow their patients out for a bit, and they all go food shopping," you told her.

Briana giggled.

For a gargantuan imbecile, Rolland could be really funny, you thought.

"You're probably right," she said as she used her white plastic fork to sort through her assortment of fruit before picking one she liked.

You watched as Briana treated the strawberry like an international delicacy, her lips caressing it with each nibble. If you were drooling, she didn't notice. But Rolland did as he stomped into the breakroom.

"Like what you see, Mike?" Rolland called out as he approached the table. Just like he did the day before, he sat down right next to Briana.

Briana looked up and saw your hypnotized eyes, and she smiled, and it was deceivingly sweet.

"How's your second day going so far?" Rolland asked.

What an idiot, you thought.

"Eh, just had to deal with a bunch of crap," Briana told him.

"Well, it's Sunday," Rolland replied. "That's the day mental institutions let their patients out, and for some reason they all decide to come food shopping."

Briana giggled again. "That's what Mike said."

"That's because I told him that." Rolland looked at you, but you focused on the PB & J sandwich in your hand, which was now down to the size of a Post-it note. "That's okay, bud," Rolland said to you.

What's okay? you almost asked as you took your eyes off the sandwich and glared at him.

Without finishing the rest of her strawberries and grapes, Briana closed her Tupperware container and stuffed it back into her paper bag. She looked up at the clock above the breakroom exit and said, "I have to get back to work." She tossed her lunch bag into the refrigerator behind your table and headed out of the breakroom, leaving you and Rolland to breathe the same air.

A week had passed, and you knew it was time to make your move. From behind the baker's counter, you watched Briana as she prepared for her break. As usual, she would say something to Joe, hit some buttons on her cash register, flick the switch that turned off the illuminated "6" above her head, and start toward the back of the store.

"Mary," you said to your supervisor, who was rearranging cakes in the display case, "I'm going to take my break now."

"No problem, Mike," she called back without directing her attention away from the cakes.

You hung up your apron, grabbed your brown paper lunch bag from underneath the far counter, and followed Briana's path. When you got to the breakroom, Briana had already begun digging into her ham and cheese sandwich. You took note of how large her bites were. Then you realized she must be rushing to get out of there, because across from her was Rolland, who lounged back in his plastic chair like a burned-out rock star. A slice of cold pizza was most likely hidden in the plastic bag that he let sit in the middle of the table. Rolland didn't make eye contact with you, but Briana smiled, mid-chew, as you pulled out the seat next to her and sat down.

"What time are you getting out today?" Rolland asked.

"Four," Briana said, swallowing the last bit of her sandwich.

"Well, if you don't have any plans…" Rolland stroked his scruff without looking at Briana. He focused on the fridge behind her. "I know of this great bowling alley in Manville, if you want to go. No one has been shot there in years."

"That… That doesn't sound too bad," she told him. "But I can't today."

"Why not?" Rolland finally looked at Briana.

"I actually have a date," she said.

Rolland sat up. "With *who*?"

Briana used a napkin to wipe her rosy lips. Then she stuffed it in her wrinkly paper lunch bag.

"Joe," she answered.

"*Joe?*" you blurted out. "The bag boy?"

"Yeah, we're going to get a bite to eat," she said, crumbling up her lunch bag. "Talk to you guys later." She stood up, tossed her scraps into the trash, and walked out of the breakroom.

You and Rolland stayed seated for several moments, neither saying a word nor making eye contact.

Then Rolland looked at you and said, "You know, this is all your fault."

"What are you *talking* about?" you snapped.

"I had a chance with her," he answered. "But you kept getting in the way."

"Yeah, okay." You rolled your eyes as you spoke.

"Seriously." Rolland looked down at his hands as he interlocked his fingers on the table. "Look at me. I at least had a chance with a girl that hot. I'm positive that these lunches with me were the highlight of her shifts. But then *you* have to come along and disrupt this chemistry we had going on. You totally made me lose the girl, and look what happened…" You waited for Rolland to finish his thought, but he didn't say another word.

"What happened?" you questioned.

"She made her own freakin' decision!"

You thought about that for a moment—Briana's *decision*. How could you let her slip out of your hands? But then what harm had it really caused? You viewed yourself as the stoic knight, but so did Rolland of himself, in a way. And you both sabotaged each other until Briana had no interest in either of you.

Perhaps you had it all wrong. You weren't destined to *save* her—or any woman for that matter. Each being is individual, regardless of gender, and this antiquated frame of mind, with the knight and the princess, can only inhibit your happiness. Briana helped you see that. Though you ultimately ended up alone, you learned an invaluable lesson.

While you sat there, pondering your intellectual incompetence, a woman you had never met before walked into the breakroom, immediately catching your eye. She approached the refrigerator and removed a blue translucent Tupperware container with the name "Diana" written on the side. She was very thin and donned long, wavy red hair that reached the bottom of her back. Her eyes were a deep green, like the basil plant in your garden that you just realized you forgot to water. With her pouty, precious lips, she smiled in your direction, but not at you. You looked over at Rolland, who was still sitting across from you, and you saw the clownish grin that stretched across his evil face.

You knew what you had to do. You had to save this Diana from Rolland, the blackest of black knights.

Thickest Thieves

Marv and May watched as Roy Davidson's car turned the corner and disappeared out of sight. The couple was sitting in their rusting, twenty-year-old Grand Marquis under the shade of a drooping oak. The car was parked two blocks down the road, and the Davidsons' front yard was barely visible through the pollen-bathed wind-shield. Marv waited a few more moments before switching the car into drive and pulling it right up to the front of the Davidsons' five-bedroom "mini-mansion," as Marv called it.

"This is the place," he said to his wife as he put the car in park.

"I thought you said it's a *mini-mansion*," May snapped.

"It is! This place has a three-car garage. And look at that tree house." Marv pointed to a wooden box with one square carved into the front. It was about fifteen feet off the ground and squeezed in between a separation in the large sycamore on the side of the Davidsons' house. A tattered rope ladder hung from the opening.

"What about it, Marv?"

"*Well*, not just anyone can own a tree house." He waited for May to nod. She didn't. "Tree houses are a rich man's game, May. That business is big bucks!"

He thought that would clarify, but May's even expression didn't change.

"Cut this nonsense out and give me the details," she said.

"All right…" Marv reached into his breast pocket and took out a pair of reading glasses. A folded-up sheet of paper was caught on a temple and tumbled out of Marv's pocket and onto his lap. He picked up the piece of paper, unfolded it, and stared it down as if he were gearing up to read the Sunday paper.

"You wrote everything down?" May shouted.

"Yeah," Marv answered. "It's just some notes so I don't forget."

"You can't write *anything* down, Marv! There can't be a paper trail." May put her hand on the sheet of paper and tilted it toward her. The name *Marv Marotti* was printed in red script at the top of the sheet, and the couple's address was printed right below it. "And look at this! You wrote this crap on your own stationary!"

"It's the only paper I use. So what?"

"*So what?* It has your name and address on it!"

"Okay, okay. I'll burn it as soon as we get home. But it's important that you know this stuff."

"*Okay*, Marv. Tell me."

Marv took a few seconds to scratch his chin before beginning. "The house is brand new—built two years ago. It's equipped with four security cameras: one out front, one out back, one by the garage, and one inside by the stairs."

"If this place has security cameras, why are we even bothering to rob it?" May questioned.

"Because if they can afford surveillance, that means they got some pretty nice stuff in there," Marv answered. "Besides, that's why we got ski masks. No one'll be able to see our faces."

"All right, keep going," May demanded.

"They have no dogs and no pets… There's a safe underneath the sink in the downstairs bathroom."

"A safe in the *bathroom*?"

"Yup. I saw it when I was installing their new toilet. It's small—shouldn't be that hard to break into. They do have an alarm system, though. But police response time on this side of town is eight minutes. Factor in the thirty seconds it takes for the alarm to trigger at the station, and that gives us what?" Marv started counting on his fingers.

"That gives us eight and a half minutes, Marv."

"Right, right. So we go in, head for the master bedroom, take some jewelry and shit, then go for the safe. Or we can split up, which might be a better option. We'll have the sledge hammer with us, and that'll be more than enough to crack it open."

When Marv was done talking, he looked over at May. She was staring at the house. The car window was rolled down, and her hair was blowing in the wind. She ran a hand through her mostly dark brown hair, and Marv could see that the strands of gray were covering more area now. Without the money to buy dye or to go to the salon, May looked years older than she did two months ago. He was sure he did too.

"We oughta take a trip, May," Marv proposed. "Bahamas. Mexico. Somewhere."

May chuckled. "I'm not interested in leaving the U.S.," she replied. "Plus, we don't have the money for it." She turned to him and smiled. "Yet."

Marv returned the smile. "We will soon, babe."

May looked back at the Davidsons' house. "So you ready?" she asked.

"Of course."

"So let's hit it today."

"We agreed we were going to rob this place *tomorrow*, May."

"I know, but I'm getting antsy, Marv. We've got all of the stuff we need with us right now. Why wait?"

"I'm not sure, hon." Marv paused for a couple seconds. "I really need to use the bathroom."

"You don't think you can hold it for an extra eight and a half minutes?"

"I don't know…"

"Let's go." May slapped the steering wheel with the back of her hand. "Let's do this right now."

"We don't even know if everyone's gone yet," Marv pleaded. "We only saw Roy leave."

"Then knock on the door. If no one answers, that means no one's home."

"But—"

"Marv, cut it out right now and pull around the block."

"Ugh, all right, *dear*," Marv said as he put the

car into drive and took it around the block, far enough away from the house so no one on the Davidsons' street would see it but close enough so that they could make it back before the police arrived on scene.

Marv took a navy blue sweatshirt out of the backseat and threw it on. Then he went into the car's trunk and grabbed two bright red ski masks and a sledge hammer. He handed one of the masks to May and tried to fit the sledge hammer under his shirt. The handlebar went all the way down his right pant leg. It made him walk with a limp, but it was difficult to notice the tool underneath his dark sweatshirt and sweatpants.

"Don't forget to put your gloves on, too," he told May. He whipped two pairs of gardening gloves out of his sweatshirt pocket and handed his wife a pair.

"These still have mud on them," May pointed out.

"Well, that's all we had at the house."

The couple walked back around the block using the neighborhood's sidewalk. Before they got up to the property, Marv and May put on their ski masks and headed for the Davidsons' front door.

Marv rang the doorbell. The couple waited a few moments, but no one came to the door. Marv pressed the button again. Still no answer. So Marv gave it one more shot and banged on the front door with his fist. After one whole minute, no one came to the door.

"No one's home," Marv said. "We're all set."

He took a step back and raised his left leg, ready to kick the front door open.

"Hold up a second!" May shouted. "You're just going to kick down their damn door?"

"Nah, see, the key is to kick near the door-knob," said Marv, dropping his leg back to the ground. "S'posed to open the door right up. Might cause a bit of damage, but that's not our problem."

"Why don't we check to see if any windows or doors are unlocked first?"

"We shouldn't spend any more time than we have to in front of these cameras."

Marv lifted his left leg up again, but before he was able to push it forward, May jumped in front of him.

"Wait!" she yelled. "We should at least check this door first."

She reached for the round, golden knob of the Davidsons' front door. She turned it and pushed, and the door swung wide open. May walked right in.

"These bastards coulda afforded a new door…" Marv mumbled as he walked into the house.

"The alarm's not going off," May pointed out.

"Probably one of those silent ones," Marv said. He looked at his watch. "9:36 A.M. right now. We got until 9:48."

"9:44, babe."

"Right, 9:44." Marv nodded. "You go for the jewelry in the master bedroom. I'll take care of the safe." Marv took a canvas bag out of his sweatshirt pocket and handed it to May.

"This is for dirty laundry," she said.

"Now it's for hot jewelry. See you in eight minutes."

Marv pulled up his shirt and slid the sledgehammer out of his pants. He ran down the hall, lifting up his sweatshirt again and revealing a pair of glasses. Then he disappeared around the corner.

All along the walls leading up to the second floor, the Davidsons had dozens of family photos with matching frames. They hung neatly side-by-side. May walked up the stairs, shifting her gaze from one photo to the next. School pictures and soccer shots became graduation photos and wedding portraits the farther up the stairs May traveled.

When she reached the top of the stairs, she looked left. The first bedroom she saw had a full-sized bed with pink sheets and a canopy. Definitely a girl's room. May shifted her gaze right and saw it: the master bedroom. She first noticed the king-sized bed with red silk sheets and about a half dozen throw pillows stacked methodically on top. She walked into the room and saw a fifty-inch flat-screen TV hanging on the wall above a dresser, merely yards away from the bed. And there on that dresser was a jewelry box about the size of a doll house. May's mouth began to salivate as she imagined all the things she was going to buy.

As she stepped toward the jewelry box, she felt a hand grab her shoulder.

"Fuckin' safe is gone," a voice behind her said.

She swung around and saw her husband, sweat dripping down his face.

"Where the hell's your ski mask?" May asked.

"I had to take it off, May," he said. "I was fuckin' dyin'. It's hot as hell in here."

"I was just about to take the jewelry."

"I got it," Marv asserted.

Marv grabbed the bag out of May's hands and swung open one of the doors of the jewelry box. Pearl necklaces, diamond earrings, and other types of expensive jewelry Marv knew nothing about were neatly arranged in various nooks and crannies in the box. He grabbed a handful, inspected each piece, and threw it into his bag, continuing this method until every item—including the box it-self—was in his dirty laundry bag.

While he was stuffing the jewelry box into the bag, he said, "Where's her fuckin' ring?"

"What do you mean?" May asked.

"Roy's wife. She's got a big-ass wedding ring." Roy took the jewelry box back out of the bag and dug through the collection in the sack.

"Marv—"

"I'm serious," Marv interrupted. "The thing looks like a fuckin' crystalized cue ball."

"Marv—"

"No, I know—I woulda bought you something like it, but I never had that kind of money. The guy's gotta be shittin' gold to afford a ring like that." Marv started scavenging through the dresser drawers. "It's gotta be in here somewhere."

"Marv!"

"*What*, May?"

"Don't you think she's probably wearing it at the moment?"

Marv had a pair of Roy's boxer briefs wadded up in his hand and threw them back into the drawer. "Damn," he said. "You're probably right. I guess we could get the hell outta here now." He looked at his watch. "9:41."

Marv and May turned to leave, but the couple froze. In the doorway of the Davidsons' master bedroom stood a little boy. He looked to be about eleven years old and had dark skin and short black hair.

"What are you guys doing in my parents' room?" he asked as he wiped his nose on his sleeve.

"Hey, buddy!" Marv shouted. "We were just leaving. Come on, honey," he said to May.

"Babe, your mask," May whispered.

"What?" Marv turned around to look at his wife and realized that his ski mask was still off. "Shit." The boy had seen his face.

May conjured up her sweetest voice and said, "Come here, hon. Let's get you back to bed so you can rest."

She stepped out from behind Marv, and the boy saw the woman in the ski mask reaching for him.

He jumped backward and screamed. Then he turned around and sprinted down the steps and out of the house, leaving the front door wide open.

Marv and May stood still for a couple seconds, until Marv said, "All right, let's get outta here," and headed for the stairs.

"We have to get the kid first!" May shouted.

"Are you nuts, May? We gotta get out of here!"

As Marv and May hurried down the stairs, they saw the flashing red and blue lights of a township police car approaching the house.

"Shit. Let's go out the back," Marv suggested.

The couple ran to the sliding door in the kitchen. Marv unlocked the latch by the handle and pulled, but the door wouldn't budge. He pulled again, but still no movement.

"*Come on*," he begged.

"Idiot, there's a latch on the bottom of the door, too," May said.

"Where?!"

"Right here." May dropped down to her knees to work the latch, but it wouldn't unlock. The door was pinned to the track.

After a few moments, Marv asked, "What's the holdup, May?"

"The latch won't budge."

"Let me take a look."

Marv kneeled down next to May to inspect the latch, and that's when the couple heard the footsteps. There were no voices, no shouting. Just slow footsteps. Someone was entering the house. Each one of the stranger's steps was slow and barely audible, but the sobering experience helped Marv and May hear every little creak and click loud and clear.

"Shit," Marv whispered. "It's probably a cop."

"Oh, my God." May was struggling to keep her voice down.

"Shhh. Keep quiet, May. Just stay calm... Look." Marv put his hand on the plastic cube that latched the sliding door shut. "Get ready to run the hell outta here," he told his wife.

The stranger's footsteps were getting louder now. He was getting closer. As he stepped into the hall adjacent to the kitchen, the footsteps sounded like a bass drum thumping on the tiles.

Marv ripped the latch from the bottom of the door, and pieces of pins and springs and broken plastic exploded all over the kitchen floor.

The slow drumbeat of the footsteps sped up. They were stomping down the hall now.

Marv pushed open the sliding door, jumped up, and shouted, "Go, go, *go!*"

May sprung up and sprinted out through the opening.

The stranger turned the corner, and Marv caught a glimpse of the man in a black police officer's uniform. The officer yelled for Marv to stop, but Marv followed his wife out the door. The couple ran down the steps of the Davidsons' deck and out into the backyard. The comforting odor of freshly cut grass was pungent underneath their noses.

They heard a voice behind them shout, "Police! Stop!" but nothing was stopping the couple's strides.

Marv and May rushed to the edge of the property as the officer closed in on them. The couple climbed the short, wooden split-rail fence and squeezed between the evergreens bordering a neighbor's property.

They heard the officer shout on the other side of the trees, but the adrenaline had taken over, and Marv and May were booking it. When they exited the neighbor's property and approached a street, they turned right and headed in the direction of their car. They peeled off their sweatshirts and gloves that were soaked in sweat as they ran toward the getaway car. When the vehicle was in sight, Marv took his keys out of his pocket and unlocked the doors with the remote. May removed her ski mask and crumbled it up with her sweater and gloves.

The couple jumped in the car and wasted no time speeding off down the street.

"Jesus!" Marv shouted. "I can't fuckin' believe it!" He turned to his wife. "We got away, May!"

May didn't respond. She just lay back in her seat with her eyes closed, silent. She held a hand on her chest.

"I can't fuckin' believe it," Marv repeated. "You know what the best part is though, May?"

"What?" she asked.

Marv reached under his shirt and revealed the canvas bag filled with all of Mrs. Davidson's jewelry.

"Holy crap, Marv! You held onto it!"

"There was no way I was letting this shit get away from me."

Marv pulled into the parking lot of an abandoned bank. He found a parking spot toward the back of the lot and turned the car off.

"Let's see what we got in here," he said. "Hopefully nothin' fell out."

Marv opened the bag and peered in, but all he saw was a hazy mixture of sparkling silver, gold, and pink. He reached into his breast pocket for his glasses, but the shirt fell faint against his chest. He looked down at his pocket. The glasses were gone, and so was the piece of paper he planned on burning once they returned home.

Marv closed his eyes and leaned his head back.

"What's with the face, Marv?" May asked. "What's wrong?"

"May…"

"Yes…?"

"You know how you like livin' in America?"

May didn't respond.

"I hear Mexico is beautiful."

"Marv… I don't want to move to Mexico. What is this about?"

"Well, it's either Mexico or state prison. You decide."

"*Marv*, what makes you think we're going to prison?"

Marv took a deep breath. "Remember that piece of paper with the details about robbin' the Davidsons' house? And how it also had my name and address on it? Well, I don't have that anymore."

"*Where the hell is it, Marv?!*" May stiffened in her seat.

"I think it's in the house—in the hallway. I took my glasses out of my pocket before I got into the bathroom, and it must've fallen out then."

"What do you need glasses to bust open a freaking safe for?!"

Marv scratched his head. "You know I can hardly see indoors without those things, May," he said.

May threw her head in her hands. "What are we going to do now?"

Behind them, Marv and May heard the sound of sirens. The cars were traveling down the road, approaching the abandoned bank. The couple could hear the screeching of the horns and sirens getting louder and louder with each passing second.

"What are we going to do now, Marv?" May repeated. Beneath her rage, she was fighting back tears.

Marv didn't answer. He was watching his rearview mirror, waiting for the police cars to pull into the parking lot and surround them.

After a few seconds, he could hear the sirens even louder. They were only a couple of blocks away now.

Marv kept his eyes on the rearview mirror. He watched the red and blue flashing lights of two police cruisers fly past the abandoned bank and out of sight.

Marv closed his eyes and sunk into his seat. "Mexico, May," he said.

"I hear it's beautiful," replied May.

Meant to Be

I am going to do it. I'm going to propose to my girlfriend. It's been two years, and I know I'm ready.

I think.

No, I *know*. I'm definitely ready.

We've been through a lot together—death of family, loss of friends, long distance—but we've come out on top every single time, and I know we're ready for this.

Take, for example, when my aunt died last month. Elizabeth was by my side almost the *entire* time. If she hadn't already made plans to visit Philadelphia with her friends, I'm *positive* she would've made it to the funeral. But she brought me back a mug with a decal of the Liberty Bell stamped on it, and I couldn't ask for better support. Right?

So I've taken her to her favorite restaurant in the city: Ristorante Marina in Little Italy. It's one of those places where the maître d' stands outside and heckles people to come in. He waves a menu at you and calls out, "Hey, come-a try our delicious penne alla vodka!" as you try to scoot by. A couple years ago he caught our attention, and we've been here at least a dozen times since.

We're through the meal now, just finishing dessert, and I don't think I can do it. Not here. There are people all around us. Every table and booth is taken. I thought it'd be cute to propose in a restaurant full of people. I'd get on one knee, ask Elizabeth to marry me, and everyone would clap and cheer as I slide the ring onto her finger and take her into my arms. But now I look around and know that's not going to happen. Not here. I mean, look at her. She's got a mouthful of tartufo, and she's going back for another spoonful. She didn't even ask if I wanted any.

I don't want to do it here. We'll go for a walk. Somewhere quiet and peaceful. Like an alleyway.

No, not an alleyway. What is wrong with me?

Okay, I just need to relax. Get through this dessert, pay the bill, and get the hell out of here.

I need fresh air. That's it. Then I'll be ready. Right?

I see the waiter walking toward us, and it eases my mind a bit. He places our check on the table. I throw down my Visa before he walks away, and he takes it.

"Oh, my God," Elizabeth says, "I am so full."

Of course you are. You ate the entire tartufo.

"Did you enjoy everything?" I ask.

"Of course! I always do." She laughs.

"Me too."

"You barely ate anything, Sam!"

"I know, I know. But what I did eat was delicious as always."

Her hand is lying in front of her on this tiny round table between us. I reach over to hold it, but she takes it away to brush the hair out of her eyes.

My nerves are acting up again.

The waiter brings back my card and says, "Have a good evening," before walking away and leaving me here alone again, with her.

As Elizabeth and I leave the restaurant and brush past the maître d', I take her hand and guide her south, right into Chinatown. That's where I'm going to propose to her. Chinatown. I thought about it in the restaurant. No one knows us there. It's far enough away from my apartment in the Upper West Side that I'm sure I won't see anyone I know. Besides, we've had fun here before. Like that one time: It was the middle of November, and she came to visit me in the city. She decided she didn't want to bring a jacket, so I had to give her mine when the temperature dropped that night. Then we got lost in Chinatown. She, at least, stayed warm during our adventure. I didn't.

Now, we stroll past a couple of Chinese restaurants and a stand offering cell phone cases and selfie sticks when Elizabeth turns to me and says, "It's getting late, Sam. I need to catch my train back home soon."

Elizabeth lives out in Hackettstown. *New Jersey*. It's a two-hour train ride with a transfer or two, and the last one out leaves at about nine o'clock. It's 7:35 P.M. now, but I'm sure tonight she'll be coming back to my apartment anyway. But I'd better do it now, before it's too late.

"Elizabeth…" I say.

She's looking at me. How are you supposed to propose to your girlfriend when she's staring right at you? Why is she looking at me like that anyway? Her right eye is squinting, and the sides of her lips are curled. She looks like the Joker.

A car lays on its horn to our left. I barely heard it, but that drew her attention.

"Oh, my God," she says.

Not here. I can't do it here. So I grab her hand, and we keep walking farther into Chinatown.

We walk past a restaurant with full roasted pigs hanging in the front window, their features clearly defined.

Not here.

We walk deeper into Chinatown. She loosens her grip on my hand and then lets go. She always does this when we're out in public—she won't hold my hand for more than a couple minutes.

We're walking side-by-side now, but I let her get a little ahead of me. I want to call her name, then she'll turn around and see me on one knee with a small navy blue box in the palm of my left hand. The right hand will be slowly lifting the lid of the box, revealing the sparkling stone inside. But, I have to be honest, it wouldn't be sparkling too much. I couldn't afford one of those disco balls the jeweler tried to sell me.

But, no, that's a terrible idea. She'll just give me another weird look if I do that.

Maybe I should just do it anyway. Get this over with. I almost don't even want to do it anymore.

So I kneel down where I'm standing, my left knee most definitely in a wad of chewed up gum that someone recently discarded. I reach into my right pocket, but I don't feel it in there. Sweat is beginning to bead up on the top of my head. I spent my life savings on this ring. If I fucking lost it, that's the end. She'll have to be happy with a Ring Pop. She'll probably eat the whole thing without offering me any of that, too.

Wait a second. I had put the ring in my left pocket. That's where it is. Thank God.

Elizabeth turns around and sees me kneeling on the ground. "Sam? What are you doing?" she asks.

"Uh, just tying my shoe, babe," I say, and I stand back up.

Isn't it obvious, Elizabeth? Why else would I be kneeling on the ground?

She's a few feet away from me now, and I walk toward her. I'm just going to get this shit over with right now. Propose, get married, have kids, live happily ever after.

With her?

Yes, with her.

"Elizabeth…" I say, looking straight into her eyes. They are so dark brown that I can't even make out her pupils.

She's giving me a weird look again. But this time she breaks eye contact with me and gazes down at her hands, which are straightening the front of her light blue skirt.

"Listen, Sam," she says. Still no eye contact. "I have so much fun with you everywhere we go, no matter what we do. You've been my best friend for *two years*."

"Elizabeth…" I say, because that's all I can manage.

"But I feel empty," she continues. "*This* feels empty. This relationship. The way I felt when we first got together… It's just not the same now."

What is going on?

She finally looks me in the eyes and says, "I wanted to wait until we got to the station, but I need to tell you now." She pauses. No more than two seconds go by. "Sam, it just needs to end. We need to end it."

I try to say something, but I don't hear anything coming out of my mouth. "No, Elizabeth, it's not over" is what I think I want to say, but I don't.

Next to us, a couple is getting out of a cab. The man helps the woman out of the backseat as she juggles her purse and a duffle bag. He catches the bags, and they both look at each other and laugh.

"I'm sorry, Sam," she says. Then she kisses me on the cheek and jumps into the back of the cab before the happy, laughing man shuts the door. I watch the cab take off and disappear within the vehicular ocean of similar yellow cabs.

"Elizabeth…" I say. "What the fuck just happened?"

But I know what just happened. I ruined my fucking pants when I kneeled in that wad of gum. That's what happened.

Bulberry Road

I pass a road every day on my way to and from work. I think it's called Bulberry Road. It's set back amongst monstrous oaks, so you might miss it if you didn't know it was there. But I know the road's there, because it rolls straight through to the east, and as I pass it every morning, I see the sun shine through the canopy of trees like a spotlight through a vacant tunnel.

I have one second each morning and one second every evening to peer down that road. From what I can tell, there are no homes governing its shoulders. It just looks like trees and open fields for miles. I feel a strange sense of solace when I pass that road, like one does when one lies down on the edge of the shore and feels the gentle pull of the waves into the ocean. Every afternoon, I promise myself that I'm going to drive down that road after work, just to see where it goes and what it's like. I expect to find acres and acres of farms and woods. But what's beyond that? I capture the road in my sight for a second, but it captures me for moments. And before I realize it, I'm pulling into the parking lot of Malone Marketing and heading up six flights of stairs toward my cubicle.

A writer never stops writing. I think I read that somewhere, in some writer's magazine. It said that even when words escape a writer, he or she never stops putting words to the page. If you write one thousand words in one sitting but only fifty are usable, your efforts are still worth it.

Since I started at Malone Marketing right out of college, I have not stopped writing. Emails.

We're a marketing firm that deals mainly with landscapers and other "yard-beautifying" businesses, and the main form of communication here is electronic mail. We do everything from radio jingles to commercials, and for the past eight years, I've been in charge of the promotional features. My boss will send me a list of clients; I will research them and then write phony review-like features to be published in bulletins, magazines, and papers in the area. But writing about manure is only thrilling for about a year or two.

I hate the term "dead-end job," but when you're in the same spot at thirty years old as you were at twenty-two, you start to recognize the term's significance a bit more. There's room to move up here, I think. The pay is decent, and the cost of living in the area isn't high. Hell, I can ride my bike to work and save even more money if I wanted to. But I don't.

My girlfriend of three years dumped me a few weeks ago, saying that I seem like I'm on autopilot. I nodded after she said that and continued to eat my defrosted TV dinner. I had no idea what she was talking about.

The highlight of my days is driving past Bulberry Road. So, yeah, I would definitely say I'm content with the way things are progressing in my life.

As I stepped into my cubicle and dropped my laptop bag underneath my desk Monday morning, I noticed a stack of papers on my keyboard. They were flyers for some company called Matt's Lawn Doctor. The graphics were terrible; the font was too small; the logo was stretched too thinly. I knew that somehow this was going to be my problem.

Down the hall from my cubicle was my boss's office. I knocked on his closed door and heard some shuffling of papers as he said, "Come in."

"Gary," I said to my boss. He was stuffing some colorful flyers into a manila folder.

"Good morning, Cooper," he greeted, without taking his eyes off of the papers in front of him. "What is it?"

"I found these flyers on my desk," I told him.

Before I could continue, he looked up at me and said, "Yes, those need to be scrapped and completely redone."

"Gary—"

"They're complete crap, Cooper. They're garbage. If I were to send those to Matt, he's liable to punch me in the face."

Gary flung the manila folder to the side and directed his attention to several memos that lay in front of him. He picked up the first two and stapled them together. Then he took a second look at them and tossed them into his trash can.

"Gary, I don't handle the content in flyers," I said. "I just write."

My boss finally made eye contact with me. "Listen, Cooper," he said, "I'm going to need you to start taking on more responsibilities here." He lowered his voice. "Don't tell anyone I'm saying this, but I think the big guy's looking to expand the company. He just bought out a firm in Trenton, which may give us a presence in Philly."

"Wow," I mumbled, not knowing what else to say.

"He keeps telling me to find a loyal number two in the office, which I'm sure will turn into something more." I snickered, and he furrowed his brow and added, "Career-wise, you sicko."

"I know what you meant, Gary." I raised the flyers in my hand. "So I'll take care of these."

I headed down the hall to Damian's cubicle. No flyer gets printed without going through him first. He was sitting at his desk, eating a clementine while browsing through Netflix on his work computer.

"Damian," I said. "Gary wanted to know what happened with these flyers." I handed him the stack of papers.

He glanced at the top one and looked up at me.

"Must be a printing issue," he said, still chewing on a slice of his clementine.

"This looks like more than just a printing issue, man. Do you have the file accessible right now?"

"No, but Leslie does. She was the one working

on it." He swallowed his food and shouted, "Leslie!"

"Yes?" The head of a woman popped up from the cubicle next door.

"Show Cooper what you did for Matt's Lawn Doctor," Damian told her. "They didn't print out right."

"Come take a look," Leslie said to me, and I walked around to her desk.

Papers were scattered all over every inch of the wrap-around desk in her space. Flyers for Green Thumb Garden, Pools & Fountains, and Sheds on Sheds hung taped to her cubicle walls in all their vibrant, colorful glory.

She pulled up the Matt's Lawn Doctor file on her computer. "This what you're looking for?" she asked.

"Yup," I answered.

The file was identical to the ones I was holding in my hand.

"Gary was less than impressed with this one," I said.

"Well, we weren't really given much to work with," she explained. "That was the logo we were sent, and since it was so misshapen and low quality, everything else had to conform to its specifications.

It messed up the font size, resolution, and other graphics."

"Can't you edit the logo?"

"We're under strict orders not to touch it."

"So no resizing either?"

"Correct."

"What if you cut out some of the copy?" I suggested, pointing to the unnecessary two hundred-word paragraph at the bottom of the flyer. "This way there won't be as much going on."

"That may work," Leslie said. "I'll try it."

"Send me a copy when you're done, and I'll explain to Gary what's going on."

Leslie gave me a thumbs up and turned back to her computer.

I headed back to my desk to get a late start on some features, but then I heard Gary's voice call my name when I passed his office. So I poked my head in.

"Cooper, get in here," he said. "Shut the door and have a seat." He motioned to the chair in front of his desk. I plopped down in the seat and immediately sank. It was missing a spring underneath, but Gary kept the chair anyway, because he said he liked it when his guests were uncomfortable. "Did you talk to Damian?"

"Yeah," I replied. "Well, Damian and Leslie."

"Tell me, was Damian eating and watching Netflix?" I was hesitant to respond, and when I didn't say anything, Gary asked the same question again. "This is off the record," he acknowledged.

"Well, not exactly," I answered.

"What is that supposed to mean?"

"He hadn't chosen something to watch yet."

"That son of a bitch. Twice already—he's been told *twice* already to get off Netflix when he's at work. He's not even discreet about it. He pushes all of his work off on Leslie and sits around eating and watching *Parks and Recreation* all day." He used his hand to wipe away the sweat that was beading up on his forehead. "I need you to do me a favor."

"What is it?"

"I need you to talk to Damian."

"What do you want me to tell him?" I sank lower in the seat.

Gary looked down at his desk. The papers he had been fiddling around with before were gone, so he reached into a side drawer and pulled out a journal-looking book. While opening it, he said, "That he's fired."

"What?" I sprung up. I wouldn't let Gary's seat consume any more of me. "Are you serious?"

"You can't be this incompetent and unmotivated and work at one of the top marketing firms in the region. He needs to go."

"I can't fire anyone!" I argued. "I don't have that kind of authority."

"Yes, you do. I'm giving it to you." He picked up a pen and scribbled something into his journal. "You're my number two."

"Will I still be your number two if I don't fire him?"

"Why are you doing this to me, Cooper?" Gary closed the journal and tossed his pen onto his desk. Then he leaned back in his throne, and I swear I saw him smirk. "Damian needs to go. And as my second in command, you will have the duty of eliminating wasteful company resources and potential liabilities—deadweight, so to speak."

"So from here on in, it's my responsibility to fire employees." I didn't realize it until that moment, but my hands were strangling the seat's arm rests. I loosened my grip and felt the blood rush back to my fingers.

"There'll also be some monetary benefits," said Gary, now grinning. "To the tune of eight percent."

I broke eye contact with him. I wanted to

smile—for the promotion and the raise—but his face was making me sick. I looked down at my watch on my left wrist. It was almost ten in the morning. Do you know how many features I could've gotten done in the hour since I got to work this morning?

"Cooper, you don't have to accept this position. No one's forcing you to do anything. Just tell me what you're going to do. Where are your priorities at?"

I was still staring at my watch. I didn't want the sight of his prickly brown mustache to sway my decision.

Without looking up, I said, "I'll talk to Damian."

"Good," Gary replied.

He might've stuck out his hand, but I refused to look at him as I got up from the seat and walked out of his office.

I headed toward Damian's cubicle and rehearsed what I was going to say to him about a dozen times in my head. Not a single one of those times sounded pleasant, but how can you make firing someone sound pleasant?

When I approached Damian's desk, he was sitting back in his chair and chomping on a

Snickers, a sharp contrast from what he was eating earlier. On his computer screen I could see Chris Pratt tossing a football with Nick Offerman. Damian hit the spacebar on his keyboard, pausing the show, and turned to look at me.

"What'd he say?" he asked me, referring to Gary.

"Well, nothing great," I replied.

Damian rolled his eyes and took another bite of his candy bar. "Of course not," he said, words lazy with a mouthful of nougat and caramel.

I didn't respond. I took the moment to soak in his cubicle. I had never really looked at his space before. It was pristine. No loose papers, no tangled computer wires, no crumbs. Even the paperwork in his "Completed" basket was uniform. And every photograph he had hanging up was bordered by the same dark red frames. One hanging photo was of him and a woman who I assumed to be his wife. They were both smiling and in their bathing suits. Behind them were scattered palm trees and a cloudless baby blue sky. Next to that photo was another of Damian and that same woman and three little children, two girls and a boy. The children looked young. They had to be under ten years old.

The photo was taken in front of a large clown head, and they were all holding putters in their hands.

"Monster Mini Golf," Damian said.

"Huh?" I responded.

"That was taken at Monster Mini Golf," he said. He had caught me staring at his photos. "It's an indoor miniature golf place, completely dark with neon lights as the only source of light. The kids had a blast."

"How old are your kids?" I asked.

"Eleven, now. They're triplets. The photo was taken a couple years ago though. It's just the two girls now."

"Did you and your wife split?" I asked. Then I realized that was too personal of a question to ask in the workplace. "I'm sorry."

"No, it's okay," he said. "Um, no." He leaned back, and his chair reclined a bit. "Benny died of leukemia about seven months after that photo was taken. That was the last birthday the three of them spent together."

I looked back at the photograph. It was hard to tell by the picture that his son was sick. He was smiling ear-to-ear, as they say, his putter held high. But the longer I looked, the more I noticed. His skin was a lighter shade than his sisters'; his eyes looked sunken; his Captain America shirt looked a size too big.

I had worked with Damian for eight years and had no idea that he had lost a son.

"I'm sorry," I said. I think he wanted to say something, but he continued to stare at the photo. "Where did you say that place was?" I asked.

"Danwood," he replied.

"Off Route 31?"

"Yeah, that's it."

"I'll have to check that place out sometime." I leaned against the entryway of his cubicle.

"It's definitely worth a trip. But don't take Route 31 if you go. There's a much easier way to get there. Take Bulberry."

"What?" I took my weight off the cubicle entrance and stood straight up.

"You know where Bulberry meets up with Harbourton Road?" he asked.

I nodded.

"Take Bulberry east for about ten or so miles," he continued.

"Wow," I said. "Long road."

Damian nodded and took another bite of his Snickers.

"How is it?" I asked.

He swallowed the candy and said, "It's fun. Like I said, my kids loved it."

"No, I meant Bulberry Road."

"Oh." He chuckled. "It's a nice road, I guess. A million times better than Route 31. Benny loved it. He called it 'Highway Heaven.' " Damian chuckled again. "I'm not really sure what he meant by that though."

I smiled, but I couldn't muster the same charisma as Damian.

"It's nice," Damian repeated. "You'll see when you take it."

"I will," I said.

He inhaled the rest of his Snickers and looked at me, waiting for me to say something else.

I held my smile for a few more seconds and then said to Damian, "Will you excuse me?"

I stepped out of his cubicle and started toward Gary's office. I stood in his doorway, making sure not to go all the way in. He raised his head and smiled when he saw me.

"Thank you, Cooper," he said.

"Don't thank me yet," I told him. "Couldn't do it."

"What?" He frowned.

"I have somewhere to go," I said. "I don't

expect to be back for the rest of the day."

I left his office before he had a chance to react. I walked out of the building and hopped into my car. My heart was pounding against my chest. I sped out of the parking lot, loosening my noose of a tie as I flew down the road. The signs along Harbourton Road glowed as I headed north. I started to see the giant trees that rested at the entrance of Bulberry Road. The sun was a little higher in the sky now, but the mesmerizing illumination peeking through those trees didn't waver a bit. I slowed my car and made a right onto Bulberry, but just past that canopy of swaying oaks sat a bright orange sign that read ROAD CLOSED.

I stopped the car. The sign only took up half of the road, so I could have easily scooted past it if I wanted to. I looked beyond the roadblock. There were no police cars or construction workers in sight, just a glimmering horizon.

I looked back at the sign. The words were in shadow, but that didn't stop the letters from radiating, taunting me. So I laid my foot on the acceleration and sped past the sign. I didn't stop for miles. I wouldn't stop until I reached the end of this road embraced by farms and trees and lakes and parks. The jet black pavement steamed in the morning sunlight. Whether it would be minutes, days, or hours, I had been disconnected from this country road for far too long, and no amount of time was going to keep me from it again.

I glanced into my rearview mirror and thought I saw faint red and blue flashing lights far behind me, but I didn't stop or even slow down.

Learn to Serve: A Guide for the Serving Impaired

*This guide is guaranteed to help you become a better waiter or waitress.**

**Results may vary.*

Introduction

Before we begin, I must inform you, as one server to another, that waiting on tables is not for everyone. If you cherish being off on holidays, serving is not for you. If you do not like working long hours with no breaks, serving is not for you. If you like spending time with your family, serving is not for you. And if you dislike being yelled at by people you do not even know, serving is not for you. So before continuing your job as a server, you must ask yourself: *Do I really want to do this?* If you *are* okay with this lifestyle—since it means you may be taking home plenty of cash each night— then you are well-equipped to begin your training as a waiter or waitress.

Part One: The Greeting

Greeting a table is one of the most important parts of your job. This is when your guests first meet you, and you always want to make a good first impres- sion. So it is essential that you introduce yourself using the name that is on your nametag. For exam- ple, if the name on your nametag is Jesse, introduce yourself by saying, "Welcome to [insert restaurant name hcre]! My name is Jesse, and I'll be taking care of you folks tonight."

Keep in mind that before or after you introduce yourself, you should *always* ask your guests how they are doing. Ask like so: "How are you folks doing?"

More often than not, guests will respond with: "Water," "Coke," or "You got any Dr. Pepper?"

No, those are not states of being; this is their way of telling you that they are *thirsty*. At this point you need to take their drink order.

Sometimes guests like lemons with their beverages. If a guest asks for one, put a slice on the rim of his or her glass. And make sure you *do not* forget the lemon when a guest asks for one. If you should forget it, be prepared for a verbal beat-down, because out of all of the tragedies that occur in this world, your guest not getting his lemon is by far the worst.

Moreover, always remember that not everyone is a fan of lemons. Recent media reports have determined that lemons can be among the dirtiest items found at restaurants. Therefore, many guests believe a dollar bill is a better drink garnish than a fruit that has been punted across a kitchen floor. Go figure.

So your best course of action is to *only* provide lemon slices to those individuals who have requested them.

Do not, however, make the mistake of putting a whole lemon in a guest's drink. That is unacceptable.

~ * ~

Part Two: Taking Orders

Upon taking your guests' orders, you must always, always, *always* repeat their orders back to them at least twice so that you have less of a chance of messing them up. For example, when your guest says, "I would like the Super Colombo Margarita Max Burger cooked medium," you must ask, "The Super Colombo Margarita Max Burger cooked medium?" to which they will reply, "Yes, the Super Colombo Margarita Max Burger cooked medium." And you say again, "One Super Colombo Margarita Max Burger cooked medium."

You will need to write this order down in your serving pad so that you do not forget it when you input it into the computer. Though it is not prohibited in most restaurants, I would strongly advise against committing a guest's order to memory. Trying to memorize exactly what a guest wants may likely result in his or her order becoming ruined, consequently spoiling an otherwise delightful evening. This is especially true if the guest isn't happy with what is described on the menu and decides to "modify" it. For example, a guest may order a Best West Dicey Spicy Loco Taco but request that it come on a soft taco shell instead of hard, have diced tomatoes instead of shredded lettuce, pulled pork instead of ground beef, extra minced onions, no secret spicy sauce, and French fries on the side instead of rice. I wish I could tell you that these types of guests are few and far between, but it is not my job to lie to you like that. Thus, in situations like this, your serving pad is your best friend so that your guests' orders come out one hundred percent correctly.

It is *crucial* that you do not mess up your guests' orders—that is the kitchen's job. However, when this does happen, your guests will still believe that you were the one who messed up their orders, which is okay, because it will only affect your tip a lot. And if you are the one who messes up your guests' orders, you must always apologize and blame it on the kitchen.

When in doubt, blame the cooks.

Part Three: Attending to your Guests

You must always stay on top of your tables. You must always be quick when guests ask you for things. You must never challenge your guests' demands. Some guests think that servers are robots, and that is just something you have to deal with. If you *are* a robot, however, you will have no problem whatsoever attending to your guests.

When a guest's drink is two-thirds of the way filled, ask him or her for a refill. Do *not* bring a refill on your own volition—sometimes guests will get angry with you. Why they get angry, though, is a mystery.

It is not uncommon for a guest to ask you for one thing at a time, making you go back and forth to and from the kitchen numerous times in a row. For example, a guest may ask you for a refill, and when you return with the refill, he will ask you for some napkins, and when you return with some napkins, he will ask you for more ketchup, and when you return with more ketchup, he will ask you for mustard, and when you return with mustard, he will ask you for some barbecue sauce, and when you return with some barbecue sauce, he will ask you for extra ranch dressing, and when you return with extra ranch dressing, he will ask you for moist towelettes, and when you return with moist towelettes, he will ask you for another refill. When your guests do this, try your best not to stab them with the butter knife. If you *must* stab them, use the steak knife.

It is unlikely that you will ever have only one or two tables in your serving section. Therefore, you will be responsible for facilitating the experiences of countless guests on any given evening. This makes it especially difficult to attend to a guest's many demands when you have more than a few tables. However, my only suggestion to you is move as fast as you can. You're a robot, remember?

Part Four: Dessert

Dessert is the best part of any dining experience. It is equally as enjoyable for you as a server, because it means that it is almost time for your table to leave.

When your guests are done eating their entrees, you must always offer them dessert by reading each dessert item off the menu. It is vital that you tell them every dessert you have, because corporate restaurants believe that guests are incapable of reading dessert menus themselves. Make sure you know *every* ingredient for each dessert, because guests will ask you difficult questions like, "The hot fudge sundae doesn't contain any dairy, right?

I'm lactose intolerant."

You may need to double-check this, but I do believe that hot fudge sundaes contain dairy.

Guests often get a kick out of asking for desserts that are "gluten free." Nine times out of ten, these guests are not aware of what makes a food item gluten free. If your establishment of employment does not serve gluten-free desserts, you are left with two options: Bring your guests any item at random, claiming it is gluten free, or politely ask them to leave and never return. If your establishment *does* serve gluten-free desserts, please quit.

Part Five: Closing Out a Check

Finally, the time has come to let your guests go home—that is, if you have not already kicked them out or made them flee in a fit of rage. This may have been the best forty-five minutes of your life, but you need to move on now.

Quickly drop the check off at your guests' table and say, "I'll take this whenever you folks are ready."

If your guest pays with a credit card, pick up the check and say, "I'll be right back," because you do not want your guest to think you are stealing his or her credit card. However, if your guest is paying with cash, say, "I will be right back with your change." And when he or she says, "No change," you are allowed to jump around and cheer, because that means you do not have to bother the bartenders for change while they are attending to their many guests. As they have easy access to cash registers, bartenders are the prime sources through which you may break down a twenty or fifty dollar bill.

Bartenders, while we are on the subject, are in charge of making a variety of alcoholic beverages, from martinis and margaritas to White Russians and Old Fashioneds. More often than not, bartenders are held to a higher standard than waiters and waitresses, most likely due to their skills in the art of mixology. It may benefit you to stay on the bartenders' good sides. The efficiency at which bartenders make your guests' drinks may vary depending on their opinion of you, and the last thing you would want to do is present your guest with a beer that is mostly foam or a Long Island Iced Tea that is mostly alcohol free. That would be like presenting someone with a gluten-free dessert, and we both know how deplorable that is.

Some Final Words

Becoming a waiter or waitress will catapult you into an environment in which you will need to channel various skills and emotions in order to successfully make it through each shift. The food-service industry hardly comes with many helpful manuals. That is why you must initially tread carefully through the various levels of serving. Now that you have examined the bulk of these levels, you are better equipped to take care of your guests and work more proficiently.

Before you finish reading, I want to inform you about one last thing: It is always imperative that you remain calm. That is key for any good server. So stay relaxed. Having a tranquil mentality will prevent you from becoming overwhelmed. A dose of apathy is fundamental when waiting tables, because the less you care, the harder it is for you to become overwhelmed. And if you become overwhelmed, you might end up stabbing someone with a butter knife, which is especially disappointing, since I told you to use the steak knife.

ESSAYS

Check the Freezer

My mom's an alien. Or, at least, she used to be, technically. So I've always admired the way her foreign brain operates. Before she could even sign her own name, she and her parents moved forty-five hundred miles to Hoboken from a southeast region of that country shaped like a boot. I learned about this when I was very young, at a time when globes were treated more like soccer balls than lavish orbs used to geographically trace one's ancestry. So I believed my mother hailed from an entirely other planet. "Italy" was either a code word or light-years away from Earth.

When you grow up believing your mother's an alien, you spend each day carefully examining her actions and mannerisms. After all, the last thing you want is to be abducted to another world before you're old enough to buy your own car. So after years of observation, I found that my mother had a particular fascination with the freezer. That's where all of the food seemed to end up. If you wanted to make yourself a sandwich one Saturday after baseball practice, you might first check the pantry for bread. If you opened the pantry in my house, you were more likely to find scotch tape and sewing tools than a simple loaf of bread.

I would ask, "Mom, where's the bread?"

"Check the freezer," she'd reply, emphasizing its location as if keeping it elsewhere would be against the law.

Our freezer was often stocked for Armageddon, and it might've been quicker for me to skip to the store and purchase a new loaf than excavate the impermeable cavern in front of me. If you stood in front of the open refrigerator for too long, my mother would nudge you out of the way, reach her hand into the fridge, and pull out what you were searching for. If her hands were tied, she'd just shout.

"It's all the way at the bottom, Patrick!" she'd say. "It's not going to jump out at you."

After a few more seconds of searching and some mild frostbite, I would eventually find what I was looking for: a smooth Duraflame log suffocated by plastic wrap, because Italians didn't buy little loaves of bread.

"Make sure you defrost it first," my mother would advise me.

This trend continued throughout my teenage years and into my adulthood, as I became a twenty-something-year-old who would still get lost inside a reach-in refrigerator. My mother would come home from food shopping with a dozen bulbous yellow bags and scatter them throughout the kitchen. She'd remove what she needed for dinner that evening and place it on the kitchen counter. Everything else that wasn't going to be consumed by the end of the day would go in the freezer.

Fish, beef, chicken, pork, pizza, butter, and even yesterday's pancakes all found their way into that industrial icebox. If you thought you might want a steak on Thursday, you'd have to know by Tuesday. Otherwise, you'd be chomping on a brick when Thursday night rolled around. Premade sandwiches for school lunches were typically buried at the bottom of the freezer, along with the expired TV dinners and forgotten bags of corn and peas. In the cafeteria, my friends would look on in horror as I unraveled my defrosted sandwich from its tinfoil straitjacket. The creamy mayonnaise would seemingly mutate into oil, turning the once-fresh bread into a soggy sponge. Just another victim of my mom's freezer.

My mother seemed to use the freezer in the same manner squirrels bury nuts for the winter. If you found a box of cereal or a bag of chips in there, you might just laugh, because that would never be as disturbing as the cellophane-bound lumpy orange blob that sat on a shelf in between an icepack and a couple Hot Pockets. Perhaps my mother received it as a gift from relatives on her home planet. For all I knew, that could've been the following week's dinner.

My mother cooked every day, so *at least* ninety-five percent of the refrigerator's contents became a meal before they were freezer-burned beyond recognition. She often cooked from scratch, and though I would put on a brave face, I always had trouble skipping dinner when I had other plans. One doesn't understand guilt until he refuses a meal made by his Italian mother, regardless of whether or not he has good reason to refuse said meal.

"I'll see you later," I told my mom one night as she lay on the couch watching reality TV.

"Where are you going?" she asked.

"To the movies with some friends."

"Eat something first," she said, sitting up. "I made broccoli rabe."

"No, that's all right. I'm probably going to have candy and popcorn and stuff when I get there."

"That's what you're going to have for dinner?" She got off the couch and headed for the kitchen. "Here, just eat a little something before you go."

"Mom, it's fine! I'll eat when I get back!" Then I ran out the door.

It is extremely disrespectful to leave an Italian's household without having stuffed your face first. If you don't gain weight by the time you walk out the door, that means they don't like you.

When I first started eating dinner at friends' houses, I had a hard time convincing my mom that I didn't need to eat beforehand.

"I'm going to Chris's for dinner," I would tell her.

"I'm making orecchiette tonight," she replied once.

"So?"

"You love orecchiette."

"I know, but Chris invited me over."

"Okay, have a little before you go. I'll start making the pasta now."

"Mom, I don't want dinner before I eat dinner…" Realizing that was the wrong thing to say to my mother, I added, "I'll have some when I get home."

"That's fine." This was how she'd respond whenever she was already directing her attention to something else. "Leftovers will be in the freezer… I'll put it on the shelf next to the Hot Pockets and the braciole my aunt sent us from Italy."

While I proceeded to crawl out the door, she might've added, "You're lucky I don't send you to live with her," but my fear of intergalactic travel was behind me, and I was now more afraid that my mother might just stuff me in the freezer instead.

Scenes from an American Restaurant

You can't really trust anything a server says. I learned that after working in a restaurant for a few years. Lots of employees like to stretch the truth or make stuff up, either out of pure enjoyment or boredom, or for another reason entirely. You really need to be careful about what you accept as truth around there, because not everything you hear is accurate. For example, if a server told you he cursed off a guest and still kept his job, you'd almost certainly believe that to be a blatant fabrication of the truth. No one would ever let even the most senseless peasant get away with such an obvious fib as that.

~ * ~

While I was in college, I worked at a popular chain restaurant that you'd know if I mentioned its name. During my time there, and even years after I left, I referred to it as the Kmart of restaurants, which isn't exactly a flattering comparison for anyone who has ever tread the sticky aisles of that decaying department store.

Serving can be mentally stimulating and emotionally taxing, regardless of who you think you are. But considering the amount of nonsense waiters and waitresses have to deal with on a daily basis, I prided myself in always being patient and keeping my cool, no matter what crap got thrown at me.

I'd often converse with the friendly clientele who frequented the establishment, but, like *all* other servers, I more than occasionally served guests who forgot I was a human and treated me much more like I was a defective WALL-E-type cyborg.

On my very first serving shift, I was baptized with one of these "tables," which is restaurant lingo for "sets of guests." Upon approaching this table, I knew I was in for an experience I could only otherwise encounter if I were to be spanked by a very wealthy widow. From the start, I was shamed by this nuclear family's perpetual frowns and sense of superiority.

"Can I start you guys off with something to drink?" I asked the family of four who could very well have been from *any* Charles Dickens novel, most notably *Hard Times*. They each ordered sodas, and I left and quickly returned with the beverages. The mother mentioned that they were not yet ready to order but that she also would like a glass of water. Moments later, as I returned with a glass of water, the dad requested a glass of water for himself, and again I came back with another. The son and daughter didn't miss the opportunity to have me run back to the kitchen, and they both asked for a glass of water at the same time. This, I learned, was my own fault, as I should've known to ask each guest individually if they required water in addition to their main beverage.

"Can you put in an appetizer for us while we're still deciding?" the mother asked after a while of looking over the menu as if it were a life insurance policy. For the table, she ordered a cheese dip that was defrosted first thing every morning. It was a franchise favorite. A few minutes later, I returned with napkins and plates for the appetizer. This was a restaurant policy for whenever multiple guests ordered a shareable dish. The mother then asked me, "Can you put in another appetizer for us? The green beans that are fried, I think. I want those." I smiled and nodded. I couldn't conjure up a genuine enough smile, so I hurried away and punched her second appetizer order into the computer, but not before scoffing at her choice.

When dropping off the cheese dip, the mother proclaimed, "We ordered *two* appetizers."

"I know," I replied, maintaining my best toothy grin. "But I put them into the computer separately, so the other one should be out shortly."

"Well, why did you do *that*?" she questioned.

Had I been allowed to answer her question with another question, I might've responded with, "Well, how are you able to dress yourself? For a person of your intelligence surely does not understand the simplest concepts of time and action." Instead, I answered, "Because I put each of them in immediately after you ordered them, and you ordered them at two different times."

She distorted her face as if she had just consumed a handful of Sour Patch Kids and then scarfed down some of that gooey cheese dip, which was my cue to leave. As soon as I walked back into the kitchen, their "green beans that are fried" were ready, the crispy batter still sizzling while the plate rested under the heat lamp. I walked the dish over to the family's table and watched the mother wave in my direction, beckoning me to come over.

"Oh, I thought you forgot about us. We're ready to order." Shaking her empty glass in my face, she added, "And more waters."

I have done intense training for races and for my own sick pleasure, but the amount of running around the family made me do that day rivaled any of it. Sometimes, if I lie awake very late at night, I can still hear their demands echoing off the walls of my skull. "We need barbecue sauce." "We need ketchup." "More waters." "Honey mustard!" "Napkins!" "Pickles!" "Waters!"

Despite the passive aggressive behavior I endured and the extensive demands I complied with, this Waste Allocation Load Lifter did not malfunction; my motherboard did not crash. I simply smiled and did as I was commanded from the moment they sat down to the moment their rich, white asses got out of their seats.

Sunday shifts are the shifts from Hell. I worked

them for a couple of years before I decided I had had enough. The Lord's Day at restaurants can be equated to children's birthday parties at the YMCA—hot, exhausting, and someone's guaranteed to cry.

While serving on Sundays, I could look forward to questions from guests like "What kind of cheese comes on the bacon cheddar cheese burger?" "Is the chicken grilled or fried on the grilled chicken Caesar salad?" and "Do you guys have water?"

On one particular Sunday, a group of five guests came prancing through the door. There was one adult—a woman who I assumed to be the mother—and four teenagers, and they sat themselves at my big "party" booth meant for no fewer than seven people. They nearly stiff-armed the hostess whose job it was to seat them.

As the hostess was bringing menus and silverware to the guests, the mother demanded five waters. The hostess let her know that their server would be right with them and walked away. Less than a minute later, I walked up to their table.

"Hi, everybody!" I greeted. "How's everyone doing today?"

"Good, good. Just five waters," the mother

once again demanded.

"Pepsi," the oldest son said. Then there was a barrage of voices, all from the mother and three of the teenagers. "Mountain Dew." "Unsweetened iced tea." "Lemonade." "Ginger ale."

I told them that I'd return shortly with their beverages and made my way to the kitchen. I had to mentally prepare myself after greeting tables like this, and the kitchen was often the place to do so. I'd joke around with the cooks, take a swig of water, stomp on a cockroach, break a glass (always unintentionally, though), but it does little to prepare you for many of the creatures who seek thrones in the slimy booths of a failing franchisee.

I soon brought the beverages to the table and proceeded to adhere to every single one of the guests' instructions, just as any good server would do. When I asked if they would like refills on their beverages, the mother told me, "Well, *I'm* not going to get it." She was incredibly rude and very proud of it, seeing as how she was unable to wipe that crooked smirk off her face whenever she spoke.

For the remainder of their visit, I didn't make the mistake of asking them again if they wanted refills, and five more rounds of them and a couple dozen demands later, the mother decided she wanted to order dessert to take home. She told me that she would like the chocolate lava cake with a scoop of vanilla ice cream on the side. "And get me the bill so I can pay while we wait for this dessert," she added.

I nodded and walked over to the computer, punching in her to-go order and immediately printing the bill. I brought the bill to the mother and walked away, returning moments later, once she had time to get her money together. The mother handed me the check with cash, saying, "The rest is for you." In other words, the cash she handed me included my tip.

"Thank you," I replied.

As I walked over to the computer in the corner of the restaurant to input the payment, another server asked, "How'd you do on the party?"

"They left me five dollars on a one hundred fifty-dollar bill," I answered, crushing the cash in my fist after counting it.

Each shift, servers tip out a percentage of their sales to the hosts and bartenders. So, at this restaurant, if someone left you a five-dollar tip on a one hundred fifty-dollar bill, you would only get fifty cents, well worth your efforts. I knew that all I had received from those guests was a few cents, and I still wasn't even done serving them yet. They awaited their chocolate lava cake and ice cream. When I remembered this, I vengefully ventured into the kitchen, caught the to-go dessert before it went out, and had a little "fun." The dessert came in two separate boxes: one for the little lava cake and one for the scoop of ice cream. I wrapped one of the to-go boxes in scotch tape as if I were wrapping a sprained ankle. Then I put it in another box, and then one more, and wrapped it again. I repeated the process with the second half of the dessert, using almost a whole roll of tape. I tossed both boxes into a to-go bag and stomped my way back to the table. I handed the bag to the mother and told her, "Have a nice day," with a big, genuine smile on my face. She didn't bother to say thank you, and I didn't really care, because I knew that once she got home she'd be thankful for nothing, which I assumed was no different from any other day for her.

I glided to the corner of the restaurant by the emergency exit, a seemingly "safe space" where servers loitered when there was nothing to do, or when there *was* something to do but we didn't feel like doing it.

I felt like I had just committed a crime. It

wasn't right what I did, but I loved how indifferent I felt as I stared down that table while they gathered their loose cell phones and pocket books and slithered out of the restaurant. It was satisfying to temporarily abandon ethics after being treated like a sick animal at the zoo. It didn't erase the events of that lunch, but for a few minutes I wasn't the loser I was every shift—or at least every Sunday.

I found myself mumbling "I hate Sundays" every week, and this shift was no different. After I said it, another server who was walking by turned to me and said, "Ugh. The shifts from Hell."

"Alright, Dane," I said, walking up to the host stand one Saturday evening. "You ready to play Crash Me If You Can?"

Dane, one of the restaurant's capable hosts, laughed and told me he would win tonight, just as he claimed every shift, but to no avail.

This game, Crash Me If You Can, was either created or refined by another server at the restaurant. She'd request to be sat with as many tables in her section as possible in a short period of time. The object of the game, for the host, is to "crash" the server, make him or her overwhelmed and on the verge of a mental and physical breakdown. The benefit of the game is that the server makes money. The downside is that he is still a server here. After that waitress was fired for stealing, I became the next masochistic server who found pleasure in playing the game, and I'd often request hosts and hostesses to try their hardest to make me crash. They were chronically unsuccessful.

On one particular night when Dane and I had willingly participated in this game, he told me, "I'm gonna try as hard as I can to crash you." If I had thought of Dane as a liar before then, that opinion was soon wiped away. That night, he not only filled my section, but he also had me take tables that were *out* of my section. Despite this busy spring night, I did not crash. Every table was content. Except one. But there's always that *one*.

"Excuse me," said the woman at table ninety-two. She had been talking on her cell phone since I greeted her—her granddaughter had to place the order—and this was the first time I got a clear look at her without a phone fastened to the side of her face. Her gray jowls hung like sandbags from a hot air balloon, and her prominent gums and teeth made her look like a county fair pony no one wanted to ride. "Can you get me a big plate?" she asked me.

"Of course!" I replied. "I'll be right back." Moments later, after traveling directly to the kitchen and back, I returned with a big plate.

"I'm sorry," she said. "This is such a mess." She was mutilating her rack of ribs, and she was getting them all over the table. "I don't even need that plate anymore… Look at this." She shoved her filthy hand holding several rib bones in my face. Small patches of meat that matched her skin tone stuck to the bones as she swung them in the air. "They're too overcooked. I'm not finishing these," she added, even though no bone in front of her had more than tiny bits of meat left on it.

"I apologize about that," I replied. "Is there something else I could get you?"

"The *manager*," she spat. She told me that her meal was so atrocious that she and her granddaughter had no desire to finish it. They tried so hard to share the rack of ribs, but neither could "stand the awful taste or smell," as she put it. I glanced at her granddaughter, who sat across from her, and it was obvious that she was far too distracted by her Leap Frog toy to care about the food. "This is why I stopped coming to this restaurant back in 2002," the woman declared before I had a chance to flee.

"I'm sorry again," I said, but I hardly was. How

could I be? A more accurate statement might have been, "I *would* be sorry if you had realized your distaste for the meal *before* sucking all of the ribs clean." But I kept quiet and fetched the manager.

Our general manager went to talk to her, and when he walked back over to me in the corner of the restaurant, he said that he comped her entire check, giving her everything for free. Surely my disapproval was plastered on my face like a gaudy billboard, because he felt the need to list each one of the woman's grievances in detail. I took too long to greet her table, and I also took sixteen minutes to get her a plate. These were a couple of her complaints, among a half dozen others.

"She's out of her damn mind," I told my manager.

He agreed. "She kept saying she stopped coming here in 2002," he said to me. "We didn't even open until 2004." He chuckled and then walked into his office.

I printed out the empty bill to show her, walked over to the table, and told her, "We took everything off for you."

"Aw, you didn't have to do *that*," she said, even though that *was* what she really wanted. "But thank you."

"You're welcome—"

"But this is a lesson for you anyway. I've been in your shoes before, I've served at restaurants my entire life—I *still* work in one—and you need to always be on top of your tables. For example, it shouldn't take sixteen minutes to get a plate."

"Huh, sixteen minutes. I don't think so. I think we should probably check the cameras for that one."

"No, you don't have to check the cameras. I timed you."

"Eh, sounds like we should probably take a look anyway." (Sure enough, after checking the surveillance footage with my manager, we found that I took just about thirty-five seconds to go from her table to the kitchen, grab the plate, and come back. It turns out that I had taken a disappointing nine minutes to greet her, but that's beside the point.)

"No, no, but what I'm saying is, you need to be more attentive to your tables. I know what it's like: Sometimes tables tip bad, and you say to yourself, 'What jerks,' or something. But take a step back and take a look, because chances are it was your service."

I told her that I understood but that I was

positive this wasn't one of those times. When she started to speak again, I cut her off.

"I don't mean any disrespect," I said, "but how many tables do you think I have?"

"Well, I can see you don't have too many."

"Well, actually, I have these four right here," I said, pointing in the direction she was facing. "Then there are two right behind you, two on the other side of the restaurant, and one in the bar area. That's kind of a lot to handle, yet all of them are content." I smiled. "Thank you for your advice. I do honestly appreciate it," I lied, "but we're on a wait right now. Your bill has been taken care of. Have a good night." Then I walked away.

Labor Day celebrates the hard-working individuals, the weariless laborers who slave away every single day of the week to provide for their families, serve their country, or both. It is a day of rest and, more importantly, a day off, except if you happen to work at a police station, fire department, hospital, retail store, or restaurant.

The thing about Labor Day at the Kmart of restaurants is that *kids eat free*. So while a server will meet some nice families on days like that, he also will meet many more of the types of parents who make Jack Torrance look like Father of the Year.

On my final Labor Day at the restaurant, I greeted my first table of the lunch rush, saying, "Hi, guys! How's everybody doing today?" (In case you haven't noticed by now, that is how I greeted pretty much *every* table.)

"Just four waters with lemon—two in kids cups," the barely twenty-year-old dad of two young boys said to me. His gremlins were climbing all over the booth. One was banging his toy car against the window. The other was testing his crayons on the walls as he perched himself at the top of the booth. The dad's better half was drawn to her cell phone.

I returned moments later with the four waters, and as I set the first one down, the wife threw down her phone and demanded, "Where's my straw?"

"I have it right here, ma'am," I answered. I set the last glass of water on the table and reached into my apron and revealed four straws, but before I could place them next to the glasses of water, she snatched them out of my hand.

The rest of the day proceeded much like that, with the junkie parents taking their malnourished kids out to a free dinner so they could spend those "saved" dollars on more sedatives for themselves. One woman was angry with me that her Sizzling Plate was sizzling. A gentleman blamed me for the amount of salt on his fries. Another woman's face turned from bubble gum pink to a Poinsettia red when her entrée was delivered only a couple minutes after her appetizer. I enjoyed a number of dizzying yet impressively fluid angry tirades insulting my intelligence, or lack thereof. Had this been a rooftop restaurant, I might have been inclined to jump off midway through table seven's never-ending "Slowest Service Ever" monologue. The highlight of my day was the guy with whom I talked football, but then he stiffed me on a thirty-something-dollar check.

Finally, at nine o'clock, after a ten-hour shift—no break, no lunch, no salvageable dignity left—I was cut, meaning I could finally go home. The only thing on my mind was cleaning my tables and getting the hell out of there. But I'd be damned if I left that place without reaching my boiling point.

As I was cleaning the tables in my section, removing the Labor Day "Kids Eat Free" advertisements from the tabletops, I heard the raspy voice of a thirty-something-year-old smoker at the table next to me. She was sitting with a man who was either her boyfriend or a hostage. My bet was on the latter.

"Oh, with these pamphlets. 'I gotta fix these pamphlets. Can't forget about the pamphlets. These pamphlets are so important!' " she mocked.

I turned to my left to see that she wasn't looking at me, so she must not have been talking about me, right?

Wrong.

Moments later, that night's shift manager, Rico, came over to her table. "Hi, can I help you?" he asked. The woman had complained to the hostess a little earlier, and she ran to get Rico.

"Yes," the woman replied. That heavy word of affirmation seemed to drop from her mouth and stick to the table like the tar that filled her lungs. Then she began her rant by proclaiming, "You know, I've been to this restaurant six times. I *never* come here. The only reason we came today was because I had a gift card." There were some inaudible mumbles as she slammed her gift card on the table. "I've worked in restaurants before," (*of course,* everyone has), "and, *you* know, it's the service that makes the place. And this place always has *horrible* service. I saw at least five employees walk by us without taking these dirty plates off our table." She motioned toward the two white ceramic plates in front of her. "You've got four hostesses up there sitting down on that bench for *guests* and flirting with the guy servers. And this guy over here," pointing at me, "is too busy with his *pamphlets* to pay any attention to us."

If there was ever a moment in my life when a switch was flipped in my head unleashing an intense fury that was solely caused by the build-up of constant verbal abuse endured in a ten-hour timespan, this was that moment. I felt like I was a five hundred gram repeater firework with my fuse lit, the spark creeping toward the base. However, I did not say a word. Yet.

My manager apologized; Satan's daughter said she'd like her check so she could leave, and Rico agreed and walked away.

After Rico was gone, the woman went on another rant directed toward her silent hostage-boyfriend, who I'm sure never went out to eat with her again. She complained about how all the manager did was apologize, how the service was f-ing garbage because the management was f-ing terrible. "This is not how you manage a fucking restaurant!" she screamed, and the heads of an old couple five tables down from her turned to see if there was an exorcism taking place.

Our hostess, Amy, walked over to me while I was cleaning one of my tables right by Arkham Asylum's next admittance. She asked quietly, "What happened?"

I responded loudly. "This friggin' bitch won't shut the hell up and is complaining about every-thing she could possibly think of so she can get something for free. She's pissed off that I'm clean-ing my section instead of taking care of her…"

Then the lady looked over at me and shouted to her boyfriend, "Now the servers are talking about me! The employees are talking about me. I can fucking *hear* them."

"Yeah, because you're being a fucking bitch!" I shouted back.

Probably for the first time since she was born, her mouth closed, and she was silent for more than a millisecond. She flipped me the bird and screamed again at her boyfriend. "Now they're cursing at me! An employee just *cursed* at me! This is why we never come here."

"Then don't fucking come back," I replied. I had been using a grimy, wet rag to wipe down my tables that night, and by this point I was strangling it with one hand. I tossed it onto a nearby booth and began walking toward the back of the restaurant.

As I was increasing the distance between the woman and myself, she shouted at me, "You're gonna lose you're fucking job! Congratulations! You just lost your job!"

"Yeah," I said, "we'll see."

And we did see. Or I did, at least. I walked into the restaurant the next night not sure whether I would be working that shift or leaving through the back door with my head hung low in shame.

When I tried to clock in, I was successful—the system didn't deny me—so I took that as a good sign. But moments later, another server came up to me and told me that Harold, our new general manager, wanted to see me. I walked to the back of the restaurant, through the kitchen, and into his office. Harold was standing next to the surveillance computer, which displayed almost all angles of the dining area. I figured he had caught me aggressively interacting with a guest the night before and was about to give me the boot. But Harold's attention was directed elsewhere. He was looking down at some papers and didn't move for a few seconds after I made my presence known.

This new general manager was an interesting

character. He was tall, and his build was some-where in the nether between skinny and profes-sional couch potato. It looked as if his skin and hair had a competition to see which could be paler. It was a sharp contrast from his almost black eyes. As far as I knew, this was Harold's first restaurant gig, which was why it took him unusually long to adjust to the most mundane tasks, such as changing the syrup for the fountain sodas and checking on tables to see how their meals came out. He was relatively friendly, meaning he never yelled, which wasn't al-ways easy to find in the world of restaurant manag-ers. I thought about all of this while I waited those endless few seconds for him to address me.

When Harold finally moved, he dropped the papers on his desk and turned to me. He stuck his right hand out and said, "I just wanted to say great job." He didn't elaborate. He just smiled, as if I was supposed to know what he was talking about. All I thought about was the night before, but it was hard to believe the restaurant had a general manager who condoned cursing off guests. So I figured this was in reference to something entirely separate.

I shook his hand and asked what I had done. Harold told me that I received a lot of great compliments from guests recently—that many of them had completed the surveys posted on their checks and wrote about the great service I had provided.

I smiled and said, "Thank you for letting me know."

He nodded and turned his attention back to his paperwork, so I made my way back to the dining room.

I hadn't been fired. I wasn't cast out like other abashed "terminations" had been. I kept my serving job, still allowed to wait on folks indefinitely and work in an environment in which I was jealous of the cockroaches hiding in the kitchen. And, suddenly, I didn't know which fate was worse.

Second Home

Three and a half years had passed before I finally left the restaurant business, but that servant mentality never left me. Some people are just born with it. From the moment they learn to walk, they instinctually wobble to the refrigerator or the cooler at a backyard barbecue, ready to fetch daddy a cold brew. But for me, I think that mentality just grew from faithfully obeying passive aggressive demands at a chain restaurant whose meals were about as satisfying as a Nicholas Cage movie. Maybe I'm not one who is always ready to serve people on a whim, but I identify with the man who spends his time behind the façade of a bar top or opposite the line cooks in a kitchen. I identify with him more so than I identify with the man whose drink is being made or whose food is being prepared. As unnatural as it felt when I worked there, the restaurant became my unwanted second home.

A year after I waited on my last table, my writing and photography services were called upon for coverage of a sophisticated golf invitational in Northern New Jersey. Fortunately for me, my father never turned me into a golfer. While most men would prefer no other environment on a warm spring day, I could list a number of destinations more pleasurable to me than a golf course. The first row in a movie theater, a surgeon's table, a family reunion—all of these would please me more than eighteen holes of expensive boredom. If I have to pay money to waste hours trekking around decorated wilderness so that I may use an anorexic stick to hit a tiny white ball into tiny white holes, I am doing something wrong with my life. However, this particular all-day event featured an array of distinguished professional athletes, so I spent the months prior to the event eagerly awaiting the day I could hang with some inspired talent. You see, for this particular affair, several rich duffers could pay a lump sum and have an active or retired football star in their foursome. The athletes would hang out in the morning, play some golf, and then head back to the clubhouse later on for a buffet-style dinner.

Anyone who wanted to meet these renowned sports figures could just walk up to them and do so. And I was antsy to do so.

I left the house a little sooner than I should have that morning. It was the only work day I could ever remember that I couldn't wait to start. That early spring morning was familiar. It was the kind when your neighborhood is a checkerboard of manicured and mangy lawns. The warmth was just thick enough so that the scent emanating from local pizzerias hung suspended in the air, even early in the morning. Consequently, I arrived at the country club a bit too early, and to keep myself looking busy, I began photographing golfers who were practicing their putts before brunch. When I finally found out where brunch was being served though, I couldn't focus on even the most talented golfer. One could've drained a putt while balancing on a single hand, and I'd have still been distracted.

The brunch was set up buffet-style. There were eggs with cheese, crispy bacon, sausage links, petite sandwiches, hearty wraps, bagels with smoked salmon and flavored cream cheeses, and a ton of other food accompanied by a variety of beverages, from milk to Bloody Marys. There was a guy making omelets and some other foreign dishes that I couldn't pronounce yet would still devour if it meant I didn't have to stick my hand in my wallet.

I took note of how underdressed I was. This was the type of event where you dressed for brunch, changed for golf, then changed once more before your sumptuous evening feast. I, on the other hand, had one set of clothes that made me look like I was taking my cousin on a date to a monster truck rally. Maybe the jeans paired with a wrinkly flannel shirt was a poor choice stylistically, but my Puma sneakers were under a year old. (I had gotten them from an outlet mall the summer before.) As far as I was concerned, I looked fancy. But then when I looked around at all these classy folk, with their Ralph Lauren shirts and their Brooks Brothers pants, I thought maybe it was a bad idea to roll up the sleeves of my flannel. Embarrassed, I considered stowing myself away under a buffet table and periodically reaching my hand out to grab some food on top of it, Dennis the Menace-style.

Instead, I stowed my camera away in its carrying case that was slung across my chest. I grabbed a porcelain plate from the end of the table and creeped my way down the spread, loading my dish with a couple wraps, some bacon, and a spoonful of home fries. When I was finished, I filled a plastic cup with lemonade. I was *disgusted* that we were expected to drink fresh lemonade out of a clear *plastic* cup, but I managed not to flip the buffet table in a fit of rage, and I made my way to the dining area to have a seat.

Behind me, at more than thirty tables, sat an ocean of men and women ready to hit the course. Experienced golfers accompanied novices who could afford to lay down a grand or two for a few hours with a famous athlete. The dining area, which was overflowing from the patio onto the country club's recently trimmed lawn, had no vacant spots. Vibrant Polo shirts and tightly knit sweater vests overtook every table. I don't need to remind you how out of place I was. Looking out at that wide expanse of royalty again, I almost felt ashamed. These were people who dressed their dogs better than I dressed myself. I just couldn't convince myself that I belonged. I had half a mind to return each strip of bacon and every square home fry back to its place on the table, inside those silver-plated mausoleums. I'd consider reuniting my stolen wrap with its severed brethren as well, had I not already taken a bite out of it.

I turned around and looked at the country club's back entrance. It was on the opposite side of the buffet. There were several small tables sitting right outside the doorway. A couple of them were covered in junk—dirty plates, used glassware—but the rest were clean. This was obviously where the "help" sat when they needed a moment to eat, collect their thoughts, cry. So I sat at one of the less filthy tables. I'm normally a relatively slow eater, but being in such a compromising space disallowed me from enjoying the taste of my food. I had finished everything on my plate and slurped up the rest of my lemonade when I heard someone call my name.

"Patrick!" a man shouted. I figured someone must have learned my name earlier in the morning, when guests kept inviting me to take their photos. I still don't know if I was right. This guy was a big, burly man. His black hair was slicked back, and he wore a loose red Polo shirt and black pants. "Take a picture of all of us," he requested, smiling. He was with six other men, all dressed alike in crisp collared shirts and pants freshly ironed by their wives.

I removed the camera from the bag and switched it on. It was an old camera and took a moment to fully start up. It took even longer to focus on the object, and since time was money to men like the ones standing in front of me, I quickly snapped some photos. I should've offered to take some more, but they had mostly scattered by the time I took the viewfinder of the camera away from my eye.

One of the men walked up to me. Over his purple Polo, he was wearing a black windbreaker with silhouettes of athletes on it. I recognized it from somewhere, but I just couldn't put my greasy finger on it.

"Patrick," he said, sticking out his hand, "nice to meet you." I shook his hand and nodded. I didn't plan on responding, which wouldn't have mattered, because he would've cut me off anyway. "My name's Jeff." He reached into his pocket and pulled out a business card, then handed it to me. "I own a few sports training facilities in the area."

I took the business card from him and saw more of the athlete silhouettes on it. He had three locations in cities I had never heard of before. I rarely came up to this part of New Jersey as it was, so I never found it necessary to learn its geography. "Nice," I said, stuffing the business card into my camera bag.

Jeff looked like he was about to deliver a pre-planned speech. I'm sure he would tell me how his business was growing "and growing fast." Somewhere in the middle of his spiel, he'd *casually* mention the famous athletes who had led clinics at his facilities over the years. "Shaun O'Hara, Darrelle Revis, *Alex Rodriguez*," he'd tell me. But someone interjected himself into our conversation, or lack thereof, and I wasn't sure whether or not to be thankful.

"Jeff!" this bald-headed stranger shouted as he slapped his hand on the sports trainer's shoulder. In his other hand, the man held a green beer koozie with a bottle of Stella poking out of it. At the time, it didn't occur to me that it wasn't even noon yet, and I'm sure it hadn't occurred to this man either. "Long time no see, buddy! How's the business going?"

I was unsure if this was my chance to slip away. I didn't want to be rude, but if I waited too long, I was afraid these men might try to sell me something. Or maybe they'd try to get me to invest in their businesses. Incidentally, I was afraid they'd just try to *talk* to me some more, and what was I to tell them? "Please excuse me. I still live with my parents. I don't belong here." And then I'd walk away.

As I pondered the possibility of fleeing the

area, two other men had joined the conversation, both middle-aged and short. They were doctors. Or at least that's what I gathered from their conversation about their "patients."

"He had a rash, and I told him it was just a rash," said Doctor One. "I told him some hydrocortisone would do the trick, but he didn't want to believe me. He was convinced it was cancer." He rolled his eyes, and the other men laughed.

"Hey, have you been down to your house in Lavallette yet this year?" asked Jeff.

Doctor One said something about the heatwave we had the month prior, but it didn't answer Jeff's question. Then Jeff's Stella-drinking buddy spoke up about his home. "I like where *your* summer house is, Jeff, but I think the way to go is to buy one in Brick. Mine's a little more inland, but it's not far from the water, which is perfect."

I was taking a shot in the dark, but I assumed that Doctor Two, who had briefly mentioned his gastric bypass patient moments before, also had a second home somewhere along the shore. If I thought I didn't belong when I was first forced into this conversation, I now was sure of it. I looked back to where I had been sitting earlier, enjoying my meal. There was a busboy resting in my spot.

Standing next to him was a server, knocking on the tabletop with her knuckles as she spoke to him. They both wore black vests overtop white long-sleeve button-downs and black pants. The attire of a waiting stiff. A year had passed since I had been in their shoes. I had moved on to covering events, interviewing notable personalities, and reviewing popular and up-and-coming destinations, but nothing had really changed. I wrote words and took photos, but I couldn't acknowledge any type of superiority over where I had been before, because there was none. There never is any. I was now standing with a group of men who owned more homes than I had lenses for my camera, but the only thing I was sure of was that I was conversing with the wrong people.

I scanned the Polo Sea of dining golfers to find some of the athletes I so desperately wanted to meet. I thought I saw the top half of the head of a former New York Giants lineman, but he was fenced in by nearly a dozen collared shirts and pleated pants, so it was difficult to confirm. The men were practically interlocking arms, and I wondered if the football star felt like a prisoner or was enjoying the conversations about beach homes and growing businesses. It felt hopeless that I might get to meet one of these athletes. But the day was long.

I focused my attention back on the group of doctors and entrepreneurs in front of me. When Doctor Two began talking about his wife's breast augmentation, I knew it was time for me to leave. I slipped out of the circle without saying a word. Since I had not mentioned my second home, I had left no impression whatsoever on them. Instinctively, I headed toward the two staff members who were conversing at my former breakfast table. I thought about jumping into conversation with them. It was as bold as it was stupid. What was I to say? "I belong here. Let's talk about our one—and *only*—home." I decided against it and swung my body right and headed for the golf course. The least I could do was take some more photos. After all, that's what they were paying me for.

Next to the practice putting green, I saw a worker arranging packages of food underneath a tent. He dropped bags of hot dogs and hamburgers on a small, round table alongside a rusting black grill. Next to him, another worker had already started grilling, and I was upset with myself that I hadn't smelled it before. This is where the golfers would be taking brief breaks in between holes.

I walked over to the tent, where some snacks were laid out, and grabbed myself a bag of sour cream and onion chips. I nodded at the man behind the grill, and he nodded back as he flipped a meat patty. The man wore a red apron, under which I could see the straw blond hair of Eddie, Iron Maiden's zombie-like mascot.

After the Iron Maiden fan flipped the patty a second time, he asked me, "How do you like your burger?"

I took a moment to respond. I was a bit disoriented by the shift in personalities of the people I had met that day.

"Medium rare," I eventually told him, surprised that he didn't just disregard me after I took longer than a split second to answer.

"You got it, bud." He threw a slice of American cheese onto the patty. "Dogs are shit," he said to me. "I wouldn't suggest trying one. We got Coke and root beer and bottles of water in the cooler over there." He used his spatula to point to the far end of the spread of snacks, where a small red icebox sat. "I got some beer stashed over here by the grill if you want some." He had a can of Budweiser in his other hand and held it up for me to see.

"No, thank you," I said. "Coke's fine." There were a few lounge chairs scattered around the tent. After I took a Coke out of the red cooler, I grabbed the seat closest to the grill and sat down. I removed the camera bag that was still slung across my chest and hid it underneath the chair.

"Do you mind if I change this crap?" He nodded toward a black boombox on a seat next to the grill. It was playing either Kesha, Katy Perry, or Nicki Minaj. I was able to tell that much, but beyond that, my ears couldn't tell the difference. I shook my head, but he wasn't paying any attention anyway. When he turned the dial on top of the radio, the speakers shot out static. The man turned the dial like a knob on a faucet, and the radio scanned through hip hop, Latin fusion, and talk radio until he finally settled on a station playing Led Zeppelin. Robert Plant was belting out the first few notes of "Immigrant Song" as the man turned the volume up on the boombox and directed his attention back to the grill. I sipped the metallic Coke straight from the can.

I thought about the guys I had met so far that day, and how comfortable I *finally* felt at the country club. After abandoning the restaurant business, a place where I'd leave part of my soul at the end of every night, it was difficult to imagine having a "second home." Maintaining a healthy living situation at two separate dwellings seemed absurd to me. I had trouble figuring out what even constituted a second home anyway. Does it have to sit by the ocean? Or can it just be the environment in which I feel most comfortable outside my own residence?

As I sipped my soda and ate my burger while listening to one of my favorite bands, I figured *this*—relaxing with greasy food and interesting characters—could be my second home. You know, until I could afford to buy one in Brick.

The Five People You Meet at Planet Fitness

I am convinced that at least half of the people who frequent commercial gyms don't have memberships there. They are simply planted in these wellness shrines as part of some twisted government experiment. Though I prefer to exercise in the comforts of my own moldy basement, I certainly cannot miss the opportunity to participate in such an experiment.

Entering the threshold of a commercial fit club can perhaps be equated to gliding through the rusted gates of an unexpected afterlife. The entrance strikes every single one of your senses, and you are dazed until the moment when you finally escape back to your car. If you are lucky, you will brush shoulders with a handful of the gym's most prominent experimentation participants, the likes of whom are staples in every commercial gym in the country.

Dress for Success

The first time in one of these commercial gyms is an experience. If you don't see a fully-dressed man goose-stepping on a treadmill within ten seconds of entering the building, it's because your eyes are closed, and I don't blame you for that. During your time spent at these gyms, you *will* see a man—a *man*—middle-aged or older, exercising in pleated pants and a button-down shirt. Though he will spend most of his time strolling through the gym, gazing at empty machines as if debating whether or not to purchase them, he will be drenched in sweat. You'll wonder if he soaked his clothes in the toilet before beginning his trek around the gym, because he couldn't have possibly gotten this sweaty from merely circling machines. But once you see him go to town on that treadmill, you'll understand where the magic truly happens. He may have brought with him a James Patterson novel or that morning's paper, but dammit, he's got that treadmill set to "speed walking," and his head's pouring like a spring evening in Seattle.

I applaud this man for his dedication. You figure he must have forgotten his gym bag at home, right? Instead of giving up on the day and going home after work, he drove to the gym anyway and began his semi-intense workout. He'd be damned if his Men's Wearhouse shirt and Chaps pants stopped him from working up a sweat. So *what* if his Tommy Hilfiger shoes cost him a pretty penny? They'll work just as well as the white-washed New Balance sneakers he left by the front door of his studio apartment. This was a one-time thing for him. Right?

Well, come back tomorrow and see that although his attire is different, the trend stays the same, and that gym bag you were so sure he simply forgot one day turned out to be fictional after all. This is what he does, and he needed that cheap gym membership in order to help him save some dough for the frequent checks he'll be laying down for dry cleaning.

~   *   ~

Cardio, Cardio, Cardio

Own that treadmill when you've got it. Own it like that last guy who just got out of work. Well, that's only if you can actually *get* a treadmill, anyway.

Cardio's good—cardio's *great*, honestly. It's important, which is why your popular wellness centers are swamped with members who only want to use the treadmill. In the beginning of the year, lines form for use of a treadmill. Thousands and thousands of miles are walked, ran, and sprinted every day on those glorious machines, and if you're fortunate enough to be one of the blessed souls who gets to use one, you'll know exactly what winning the Powerball is like.

The person running on the machine next to you is most likely wearing a headband, short-shorts, and a one-size-too-small long-sleeve shirt from his alma mater. If I'm right, you just hit the jackpot. This guy—and his girlfriend, who definitely is on the other side of him—knows *everything* there is to know about fitness. Ninety-eight percent of that knowledge consists of exercises that involve strictly cardio, but hey, it's better than nothing.

Don't pay your gym extra for a personal trainer. Instead, get in line in the beginning of

January, and have one of the treadmill jockeys coach you on how to lose that stubborn belly jelly and get back into the shape of a well-formed oak tree branch. If they don't say the word "cardio" at least seventy-two times within the first hour, check a different machine in the lot, because this guy knows nothing.

You don't need to bench, squat, deadlift, or do even a single sit-up. The only time you'll ever do a push-up is after you've fallen down from exhaustion. It may sound too good to be true, but that's just the life of a cardio junkie, and once you've met one, your life will never be the same.

However, these people seem to forget who you are moments after you've stopped speaking to them. If you see them again the next day at the gym, you'll be just another stranger who doesn't know how to work out, and they'll feel the need to introduce themselves again.

"My name's Trevor," he'll say to you as he increases the incline on his treadmill. "This is really important to do right before the cardio cooldown. *Really* important. I came up with the theory myself. Cardio is really important."

"I know. You told me all of this yesterday," you may remind him. But much like a Yorkshire terrier, he will keep yapping instead of listening to you.

"Cardio is really important," he'll repeat. "It strengthens your heart and lungs and increases your bone density and helps you lose a tremendous amount of weight. It also makes you feel better."

If he doesn't start tinkering with your machine for you, just wait a tad longer; first, he has to tell you about his weight-loss journey and all of the trials and tribulations that led him to becoming the fitness guru he is today, paying ten dollars a month to run on a conveyer belt six times a week. Pure genius.

This Machine is My Recliner

Whether or not you actually want to exercise at a health club, it goes without saying that you do not need to stay home.

Let me rephrase that.

Affordable commercial gyms come equipped with intricate recliner sofas, and since these facilities are also lined with flat-screen TVs, you certainly don't need to stay in your living room to relax and see who CNN and Fox are blaming now.

Many members of these gyms take full advantage of that fact.

The benefit of treating exercise equipment as fully-fledged Sleepy's furniture is that you won't work up a sweat. So wear whatever you'd like, but the combination of a pair of sweatpants and an ill-fitting T-shirt is the universal sign for *I don't want to be here right now*. So go with that.

The chest press machines are often situated directly in front of the flat-screen TVs that hang along the center of the gym like damp clothes on a laundry wire. The chest presses are basically cushioned seats and should be treated as such. Check those out when you visit. You'll surely see someone scrolling through Facebook on his phone instead of building the muscles in his biceps, triceps, and chest.

The lat pull-down machines yield the same results, as most folks are ecstatic to find a comfortable place to lean forward in their seats, phone in hand, instead of mimicking a pull-up in benefit of the broadest muscles in the back.

Maybe you fancy somewhere to lounge, for which I present you with the horizontal seated leg press, or the "rowing machines." This is where you can easily plant your butt, cross your legs, and break out that bag of potato chips while you watch all the other suckers redden in determination on those "useful" machines.

I've seen that only once, although the gentleman must have already finished his chips, because they were nowhere to be found. Instead, his ears were plugged into the cellular device he held in his left hand, and in his right I could've sworn I saw a remote control, which he used to change the Food Network to TV Land on the television above him. Had I walked up to him and asked to use the machine, he might've replied, "This machine is my recliner," and I would've felt like a fool to impose.

There's a Hole in the Fence Out Back

There are some people who obviously don't belong at the gym. I don't mean the people who have years of hard work ahead of them before achieving their goal (a goal which never arrives for even the most affluent athletes, mind you). No, I am talking about the people who clearly snuck in when the employees' backs were turned. They arrive fully dressed in their workout attire and leave the exact same way, no trips to the locker room or even the lavatories. I am positive that the gym staff does in fact see these bozos creep in, but they don't care enough, and certainly are not paid enough, to put up a fight.

I've made the mistake of people-watching at the gym, which has allowed me to gather insight on all of the species of human who congregate inside an institution such as this. If I had to attribute each species to a creature in the animal kingdom, I'd call these trespassers rabbits. The speed at which they ricochet from machine to machine is impressive. One moment they are curling dumbbells, the next they have the StairMaster cranked up all the way and are stomping up the steps at a rate that would put Bugs Bunny to shame, even during wabbit season. Perhaps those who sneak into these gyms believe that they stick out like sore thumbs to the staff and are bound to get caught if they do not move fast enough. This would explain why they never spend more than thirty minutes inside the establishment.

When it's time to go, when they're drenched in as much sweat as the guy reading *The New York Times* on the corner treadmill, they leave just as stealthily as they arrived: Water bottle clutched in his fist, the gatecrasher crouches beside the elliptical. He looks to his right. At the front counter, three employees converse while staring down at their mobile phones. When they are deep in "conversation," or, conversely, more interested in Brittney's Instagram selfies and Ben's most recent anti-gun rant, the intruder makes a break for it. He sprints to the front door, and before the staff even hears the ding at the entrance, the rabbit is down the road and heading for his hole.

I "Know" What I'm Doing

I know what I'm doing. I don't need anyone to tell me otherwise. In fact, in conversations outside of the gym, I always make sure it's obvious that I *think* I'm well-versed in fitness. In reality, I nearly flunked out of biology. But in my defense, I was never very good in *any* type of science.

I always pack a worn-out band T-shirt, prefer- ably classic rock, and mismatch it with a pair of those thin shorts with the fluorescent compression briefs stitched underneath. I've got tube socks worn high above my Nike kicks, and my Fitbit is cutting off the circulation to my hand. So when I step over to the Smith machine and start loading the bar with tens, I'm preparing for an intense workout that impresses no one but myself.

I'm not the only one; we come in all shapes, sizes, and ages. We're too good for the powerlifting gyms, where men and women are chalking up their palms, benching four-times their bodyweight and screaming while they do it. No, we don't *need* to scream. In fact, we're not even allowed to. We might get kicked out of the gym for it. So if you ask me why I never sit deep into my squat, that's not the reason why, but it might as well be. If I don't touch the bar to my chest every few reps when I'm benching, it's because I'm working on a new technique.

I know exactly how to use the machines and never need to consult the helpful diagrams located alongside them. They leave vital steps out of those diagrams anyway. For example, the most important thing to do after every set is to scan the gym to see if anyone was watching you. If you *are* being watched, chances are it's by an elderly man who is massaging the seat of the chest press with a paper towel before taking a load off. But never forget to look around after every set anyway, just in case that attractive girl in the cardinal red leggings quits looking at herself in the mirror long enough to notice you bench your weight. Or maybe you prefer her boyfriend who's curling forty pounds while texting. I'm sure they both are thrilling conversationalists once you get to know them.

The mirrors are there for your benefit, just as they are there for the benefit of the egocentric gym varmints, who, I am convinced, only get gym memberships so that they can look at themselves in public. Every once in a while, they will begin to work out their muscles, though. Those who do almost certainly have a spec of plastic in one ear that is transmitting signals from the nearest cellular tower. These are always men, and it may be his wife on the other line, telling him to stop at the grocery store on his way home. Or maybe it's his mistress begging to hear the sounds he makes while he's working out. But, most likely, the poor soul on the other line is a friend he doesn't particularly care for. I assume that this gym member decided to make the call as soon as he hit the Smith machine so that his "friend" is subjected to half-breaths and periodic fluffy grunts for the better part of an hour.

"I need to get more whey protein," you may hear him say into his Bluetooth earpiece as he stares into the mirror and pets the top of one of his biceps.

I utilize these same mirrors (though I always leave my Bluetooth earpiece at home and forget to pet my scrawny arms). When I squat, I watch my eyes begin to cross and my face turn red, and I know it's time to remove a ten and replace it with a two-point-five. If I'm being watched, I need to be presentable.

It's all right to record yourself while lifting in order to showcase your expertise. But if you don't post the video to social media, it never happened. These momentary recordings chronical your victories just as easily as they do your struggles.

You will never see me struggle when I'm working out, however. That's simply because I don't push myself. Why bother? When my armpits start to get damp, that's when I know it's time to leave. I wore my favorite band T-shirt, and there's no way in hell I'll ruin it with unwanted perspiration. Besides, this is my only pair of workout shorts, and I need them again tomorrow. Also, I've been thinking about dinner the whole twenty minutes I've spent at the gym, and it's just about time I satisfy those cravings.

Dozens of signs around the gym advise me to wipe down the equipment after using it, so I grab a fistful of paper towels, spray the equipment down with some antibacterial composite, and use that to cleanse the expensive machinery. The next time I come back to the gym, I'll utilize the same equipment and complete the same workouts. Every new day is a reflection of the last. Certain machines remain out of my sight so that I can focus on the ones that truly matter. I work out the same muscles and yield the same results day after day. I may not look like I've made any "real" progress, but that is purely because I am doing everything correctly. After all, I *know* what I am doing.

Support Local Music

I'm really into indie music. There's a fervent energy within the independent music scene that is lost at your typical sold-out arenas. In these intimate settings, twenty-five people can summon as much fire and fury as the twenty-five thousand who are surfing the web on their mobile phones at a Skrillex concert. Indie shows are often in-your-face intense, and everyone in the audience *shows* their engagement, either by dancing, head-banging, or accidentally knocking someone or something over. I'm usually the guy hiding behind a used Nikon, though—the one who creeps to the middle of a small group, snaps a photo of the performing band, and scurries away, not to be seen until the next band takes the stage. But I always enjoy an indie show, regardless of my phantom tendencies. At most, it is an opportunity to connect emotionally with true, unencumbered artists whose boundless nature allows them to thoughtfully and thoroughly share what's secluded in the deepest fissures of their tumultuous minds. At least, it gets me out of the house.

A lot of the time, learning about the musicians and their backgrounds and inspirations is just as enjoyable as their distinctive tunes, and I never miss an opportunity to get to know more about these artists and what they are into. Their interests and ambitions and histories and desires extend way beyond the connotation of the pot-smoking punks and hipsters who grace made-for-TV movies. They're different, complex people. Every single one of them.

The indie music scene in New Jersey is one of the most diverse you will find. It features some of the most talented and knowledgeable artists you've never heard of and, frankly, probably never will. That does not diminish their quality or determination, but judging by the immensely tough competition in this field, as well as America's insatiable appetite for stellar piles of musical feces, this talent may appear wasted. However, the skills of these musicians are not wasted; they're very much utilized to produce soulful, authentic tunes you will never *feel* anywhere else.

I was a college student when I found out that one of my coworker friends was in a band. I had friends in high school who wrote music and performed as often as a teenager's schedule and strict curfew would allow, but I never actually went to see them play. I always told myself I ought to see one of their shows, but I hardly ever listen to myself as it is, and I was still reluctant to listen then. I frequently played sports and hung out with my friends, but that didn't mean I'd choose going out over locking myself in my room and reading if I had the option.

One of the first shows I sat through the entirety of was in the basement of a church in my hometown. Maybe it was the divine presence that guided me out my front door that evening, or maybe it was my friends begging me not to skip another show. Whatever it was, it overpowered my desire to dig into another David Sedaris book, and I found myself at church on a Saturday night, praying for "just one more song."

The show introduced me to several cool acts, and I made a point to attend a number of future humble performances throughout the years, whether I was acquaintances with the bands or not.

New Jersey hotspots for this genre are New Brunswick, Asbury Park, and Hoboken, but that doesn't stop the entirety of the state from rocking out every Friday and Saturday night. There are shows all year round, and with Philly and New York just a couple highways away, you will never have trouble finding some indie shows for the weekend.

New Jersey bands regularly travel out of the tri-state area to perform for small audiences who dig the east coast flavor, but you'll also find a plethora of bands from the other forty-nine states coming to our neck of the parkway. You may lie in bed and listen to music by artists from other states, but until you stand five feet from a Midwestern boy screaming his heartache into a broken microphone, you don't know squat about your fellow countrymen. The experience is different, because it *comes* from somewhere different and it's presented to you in a respectable setting, as opposed to a sort of artificial environment created from expensive recording equipment. These out-of-area artists present new ideas and philosophies, which are facilitated by an almost foreign dialect. Their vernacular is familiar yet unrecognizable at times. In other words, they're usually *friendly*. If you are introduced to these friendly artists, you'll spend a decent portion of your time carefully picking out your words so that you don't inadvertently offend your new friend with traditional New Jersey terms and phrases that are considered rude in normal societies.

On one of these occasions, I made a friend from Nebraska who had recently swam in the Atlantic Ocean down in Cape May, despite February's frigid weather.

"It's different for you guys," he told me, "because you're always right by the ocean, so it probably seems like no big deal. But in Nebraska, we're right in the middle of the country and rarely come out this way. So when we're by the water, we don't miss an opportunity to jump in."

We got to talking about his band and their past tours and what he does to fund these mini laps around Uncle Sam's melting pot. Then he asked me a simple question in an effort to get to know *me* better: "What are you into?"

What am I into? I wasn't sure how to answer that. It was easy enough to figure out. Television and dessert—that's what I'm into. I also enjoy yelling at malfunctioning technology, saying the opposite of what people want to hear just to get a good laugh at their frustration, and doing absolutely nothing whether or not it's convenient. I've watched *The Office* at least ten times through and own all seven seasons of *Boy Meets World* on DVD. I've had turtles for nearly two decades. I stack boxes of books and comics by my bedroom window. I keep a yardstick next to my bed so that I can shake my ceiling fan when it starts to make that insufferable rattling sound. (It usually helps to make the rattling go away.) But what am I *into*? I continued to list my likes and habits in my head, but I knew this wasn't what he was asking about.

Did he mean what do I do—like, for a living as well as in my free time? But he asked the question way too politely, and it caught me off guard. Us northeasterners ask, "What do you do?" as if it's an accusation rather than genuine interest in someone's employment or hobbies. We'd ask it in the same manner a boss would ask a subordinate if he was stealing, or in the same way a mother would reprimand her child for misbehaving at school. "Are you happy with yourself?" the mother would ask her middle school son who had just pulled the fire alarm, and he'd bow his head in a shameful silence, just as I might if a New Jerseyan asked me, "What do you do?" But Midwesterners found a way to ask that same question politely, and naturally rude New Jerseyans have no way to answer without returning a discourteous response out of force of habit.

So, as I continued to ponder his question, I chuckled and looked toward the exit. I scratched the back of my head. *What the hell do I do? What am I into?* "I write," I thought about answering, but that wasn't what he was looking for, was it? So, instead, I said, "Ah, you know…" and my voice trailed off. We stood in silence for a few more moments while he awaited a response that never manifested. Soon he said goodbye and walked away. That was the last I ever saw of my Nebraskan friend, and sometimes I wonder if he's still waiting for my answer.

I've never been asked that question by a New Jersey musician, but considering that my days of enjoying indie shows are not over, I've learned to prepare myself for future questions asked by naturally polite out-of-staters.

"What are you into?" I may be asked again one day.

Now, I'll respond, "I'm into supporting local music," and I'll return a friendly grin and tell him all about the diversity of New Jersey's indie music scene as he respectfully smiles and nods his head and learns about what I'm into, regretting that he ever asked.

ABOUT THE AUTHOR

Patrick Lombardi is a life-long New Jersey resident. He studied English at Rider University before beginning a career in writing and journalism. He currently contributes to BestofNJ.com and works for the state. This is his first publication.

patricklombardi.com

Printed in the USA
CPSIA information can be obtained
at www.ICGtesting.com
LVHW070328130923
757994LV00002B/254